# SPIRITS OF
# SAN FRANCISCO

BY THE SAME AUTHOR

**GARY KAMIYA**
*Cool Gray City of Love: 49 Views of San Francisco*
*Shadow Knights: The Secret War against Hitler*

**PAUL MADONNA**
*Come to Light*
*Close Enough for the Angels*
*On to the Next Dream*
*Everything is its own reward*
*All Over Coffee*

# SPIRITS OF SAN FRANCISCO

## VOYAGES THROUGH THE UNKNOWN CITY

GARY KAMIYA
DRAWINGS BY PAUL MADONNA

BLOOMSBURY PUBLISHING

NEW YORK · LONDON · OXFORD · NEW DELHI · SYDNEY

BLOOMSBURY PUBLISHING
Bloomsbury Publishing Inc.
1385 Broadway, New York, NY 10018, USA

BLOOMSBURY, BLOOMSBURY PUBLISHING, and the Diana logo are trademarks of
Bloomsbury Publishing Plc

First published in the United States 2020

Bloomsbury Publishing Plc does not have any control over, or responsibility for, any third-party
websites referred to or in this book. All internet addresses given in this book were correct at the
time of going to press. The author and publisher regret any inconvenience caused if addresses have
changed or sites have ceased to exist, but can accept no responsibility for any such changes.

ISBN: HB: 978-1-63557-588-0; eBook: 978-1-63557-589-7

Library of Congress Cataloging-in-Publication Data is available

2 4 6 8 10 9 7 5 3 1

Designed and typeset by Elizabeth Van Itallie
Printed and bound in the U.S.A. by Berryville Graphics Inc., Berryville, Virginia

To find out more about our authors and books visit www.bloomsbury.com and sign up
for our newsletters.

Bloomsbury books may be purchased for business or promotional use. For information on
bulk purchases please contact Macmillan Corporate and Premium Sales Department at
specialmarkets@macmillan.com.

TO OUR FAMILIES

# CONTENTS

# DESERTED CITY OF THE HEART

## HOW I LEARNED TO LOOK AT SAN FRANCISCO UNDER QUARANTINE

THE MORNING THAT San Francisco went under quarantine, I walked out my door with my dog and headed down to Washington Square.

North Beach was a tabula rasa. A stage set for a play with no characters. A de Chirico painting come to ghostly life. The collective fantasy of every San Franciscan who has ever tried to get onto the Bay Bridge on Friday afternoon at five P.M.

It was bizarre and disquieting, and clean and otherworldly. And I found it intoxicating.

This feeling was due, in part, to personal circumstances. I had had one of my artificial knees replaced two and a half weeks earlier, just getting under the wire before the city banned elective surgeries. When Mayor London Breed issued her shelter-in-place order on March 16, I had only been back in my Telegraph Hill apartment for six days. I was still in pain and having trouble sleeping, but I was doing physical therapy, was getting stronger, and walking a little farther every day. I was grateful that I could walk. And I was overjoyed to be walking through my city.

In *The Gay Science*, Nietzsche, most of whose adult life was filled with agonizing physical pain, wrote a magnificent description of the experience of returning to health. "Gratitude pours forth continually, as if the unexpected had just happened—the gratitude of a convalescent—for convalescence was unexpected. 'Gay Science'—that signifies the saturnalia of a spirit who has patiently resisted a terrible, long pressure—patiently, severely, coldly, without submitting, but also without hope—and who is now all at once attacked by hope, the hope for health, and the intoxication of convalescence."

Regaining my health explained part of my euphoric reaction to this brave new San Francisco without people in it—but not all of it. Even if I had not been recovering from surgery, I'm sure I would have felt the same exhilaration.

I'm not alone. All around the world during this pandemic, people have had similarly complex, and often positive, reactions to their suddenly and strangely silent cities. They report feeling unsettled, disturbed, awestruck—and peaceful, calm, even joyous.

There's no great mystery why. Everyone in a suddenly empty city sees it with fresh eyes. No one would want the experience to come at such a terrible cost, but the surreal, deserted cities that were created by the Covid-19 virus jump-started a million dormant synapses. If cities are works of art, then the pandemic transformed them from conventional figurative paintings to transgressive modernist ones, transformed by what the art critic Robert Hughes called "the shock of the new."

We are all always searching for the shock of the new. The desire to see things, including cities, afresh is hard-wired into us as humans. It's why we make art, play music, write books. Indeed, it's the whole point of this book. In our different ways and mediums, Paul Madonna and I are trying to portray a San Francisco that is rich, deep, and strange—an unknown city.

Others trying to shake themselves and their city out of their torpor take a more aggressive approach. From ur-flaneur Charles Baudelaire through the Parisian Situationists, the London psychogeographers, San Francisco's own Suicide Club, Cacophony Society, Worst Party Ever, and beyond, there's a long modernist tradition aimed at the derangement and defamiliarization of place. I've been on a number of weird urban explorations organized by some of these groups, and as I walked around through the quarantine city, I couldn't help but think that seen as a culture jam, it was stupendous. What an event! Eight hundred and ninety thousand people stayed home for seven weeks and counting? Now *that's* a flash mob!

But beyond the joy of my recovery and the otherworldly frisson of the deserted streets, there was a deeper, more familiar reason for my intoxication: San Francisco's sheer physical beauty. City dwellers rush to nature to get away from the depressing realities of the coronavirus; in San Francisco you can do that by opening your front door.

As a result, you don't notice the quarantine as much here as in other cities. New York is an utterly human hive: an empty Broadway violates the essence of the city. In San Francisco, a deserted street seems to open a window to the place's deepest heart. The sublime terrain tends to swallow up everything else, including people. The hills, the bay, the sky, the sea are constantly overpowering the human one here. Down any street, some unknown hill or patch of mysterious water appears in the distance, and everything else arranges itself around that enticing mystery. Every street is already a de Chirico. There is something that feels sublimely empty about this city even when it's full of people.

Writers have always noticed this. William Saroyan wrote, "The Pacific has a lot to do with the temperament of San Francisco. The city is literally of the sea. It has everything. Sea, earth, sky, and the world." In *The Heart Line*, the author and editor Gelett Burgess celebrated what he called San Francisco's "topographical chaos": "No other city has so many points of view, none allures the stranger so with coquetry of originality and fancy. Some cities have single dominant hills, but she is all hills, they are a vital part of herself. They march down into the town and one cannot escape them . . . the San Franciscan is always in San Francisco, the city of extremes." In *I Know Why the Caged Bird Sings*, Maya Angelou described how for her as a thirteen-year-old black girl, "the city was a state of beauty and a state of freedom . . . I became dauntless and free of fears, intoxicated by the physical fact of San Francisco." By contrast, the people she saw "were at most gilt on the frame of my portrait of the city." The poet George Stirling simply wrote, "At the end of our streets the stars." And stars trump streets.

Being in a city so open to the universe made the quarantine feel very far away. As I walked up to Coit Tower at sunset and looked out at the red ball of the sun dropping behind the Marin Headlands, with the Golden Gate Bridge looming over the velvet bay, it was hard to remember that San Francisco was even locked down and facing a terrible threat.

Of course, it was and is locked down, and it is still facing that threat. Mercifully, because it shut down early, and perhaps for other yet-unclear reasons, it has so far escaped the horrors visited upon New York City, Detroit, New Orleans, and so many other American cities. As of May 5, San Francisco, population 880,000, has had 1,624 Covid-19 cases and 29 deaths. By comparison Manhattan, population 1.6 million, has had 22,900 cases and 2,220 deaths. It is infinitely easier for a San Franciscan wandering around under quarantine to enjoy the experience than a New Yorker.

But even though we may have gotten off comparatively easily, there are still people suffering and dying here, and thousands of people out of work and unable to pay their rent, and beloved small businesses closing, and doctors and nurses and other front-line workers risking their lives to do their job, and bus drivers and grocery clerks and cops and all the other people keeping the machinery of the city running so that people like me can wander around and look at the views. In the midst of such a crisis, sniffing the metaphysical perfume of your city's mysterious and melancholy streets could be seen as precious, clueless, and callous.

Actually, I don't think there's anything wrong with enjoying yourself in whatever way you want to in your city, whether it's under quarantine or not. As long as you're not acting irresponsibly and endangering anyone else's health, why not? Being a flaneur doesn't harm anyone, unless the guy across the street from you is irritated by your too-too Oscar Wildean sighs.

But recently I did have to sit down and have a conversation with myself. It's one thing to enjoy having the city all to oneself. It's another to get irritated when people start taking it away. And to my chagrin, I did just that a couple of days ago, when warm weather, the flattening of the curve, and cabin fever led hordes of San Franciscans to emerge from sheltering in place and pour all over my favorite haunts.  I found myself thinking, "How dare these plebian interlopers profane my solitude!"

At that moment, I realized maybe I'd been alone too long. Being a writer makes it easier to be under quarantine—hell, we're always locked down, all we do is sit at home working all day anyway. But it also exacerbates some introverted tendencies I have, not all of them particularly healthy, and under their malign influence I realized I had begun to emulate the narrator of a certain Simon and Garfunkel song. It was all well and good to use the opportunity of the streets being deserted to commune with the rocks on Telegraph Hill Boulevard. But I didn't want to turn myself into a rock.

Luckily, it wasn't hard to break out of my metamorphic malaise. Just walking around and looking at all the empty and boarded-up storefronts did the trick. Yes, I love San Francisco's natural beauty. But I love Caffe Trieste just as much, and the crowd of tourists at the Powell Street cable car turnaround, and the Chinatown branch of the library, and SF Jazz, and friends I can actually visit in their homes, and the motley line of Latinos and Google employees at El Faro, and the congeros at Hippy Hill in Golden Gate Park, and Union Square on a sundress day, and City Lights at eleven P.M., and Market Street with its holy eternal grifters, and the tabletop jukeboxes at Gaspare's, and jazz night at Spec's, and the six-egg shrimp dish at Yee's, and the Castro Theater, and opening night at the opera, and the upstairs booths at Vesuvio, and miraculous Aquatic Park, and all the other unnecessary and divine things that humans have created here. Take those things away, and San Francisco really would be just an exquisite, lifeless stage set. Stars don't really trump streets. You need them both.

I badly want that living city back. But not until it's safe.

Making it safe, of course, is what we've all been doing for the last seven weeks. That's the reason the streets are empty. And lately, as I take my walks through those not-quite-so-deserted streets, it has occurred to me that my city and I share something. We're both convalescing. We're both doing physical therapy. We're both on an upward path.

And so as I walk through San Francisco these days, or sit in my apartment, I see a different kind of beauty than I did at first. Not just the desolate beauty of the city's empty streets, or the ageless natural beauty that is her birthright, but an invisible one: The beauty of her people, locked down inside their doors. Staying the course. Saving their city.

In his meditation on convalescing, Nietzsche wrote of "a reawakened faith in a tomorrow and the day after tomorrow, of a sudden sense and anticipation of a future, of impending adventures, of seas that are open again, of goals that are permitted again, believed again."

As we stand shoulder to shoulder in our separate homes, our goal is coming in sight: rebuilding our city. And that goal—and that unity of purpose—is more beautiful than any view in San Francisco.

Gary Kamiya
Varennes Street
San Francisco
May 5, 2020

# INTRODUCTION

When I was a kid, I was fascinated by a 1957 book by the Dutch author Kees Boeke called *Cosmic View: The Universe in 40 Jumps*. The book opens with a photograph of a girl holding a cat and sitting in a desk chair, seen from about five meters up. The second image shows the same girl, but from a vantage point ten times farther away from her than the initial one. The girl is now quite small; establishing the scale are drawings of three objects near her: two cars and, weirdly, the front half of a blue whale. The third image is ten times higher up than the previous one, or five hundred meters; the girl has become a speck, and you can see the cars, the entire whale, a courtyard, a U-shaped school building, and a road outside it. The fourth image is ten times higher, or five thousand meters; the girl has completely disappeared, the whale is barely visible, and the edges of a village can be seen. The fifth image, from fifty kilometers, shows a big city and the surrounding countryside. The sixth image, from five hundred kilometers up (310 miles), shows central Holland. The seventh image, from five thousand kilometers, shows much of Western Europe, including fifteen different countries. The eighth, from fifty thousand kilometers (about thirty thousand miles), shows the entire planet Earth. In the ninth, from five hundred thousand kilometers, or 312,500 miles (more than the distance to the moon), the Earth has become a small globe far below. Not until the fourteenth image can the entire solar system be seen. The last image in the sequence, number twenty-six, shows countless galaxies, each of them a tiny dot, one hundred million light–years away from the girl.

Those twenty-six jumps zoom away from the girl. The next fourteen zoom in. The first image is the familiar photograph of the girl, with a small square focused on the hand holding the cat. In the second, the vantage point is just a few inches above her hand, and a mosquito feeding on her is clearly visible. In the third, we are only five centimeters above her hand, and water mites can be seen on her flesh.

In the fourth, from five millimeters up, a bacterium has become visible. And so the jumps inward continue, at greater and greater levels of magnification, until we come to the final image, the nucleus of a sodium atom—in 1957, the frontier of our scientific knowledge.

As I was researching and writing this book, I sometimes thought about *Cosmic View*. For cities are entities, like the little girl holding the cat, and you can choose to get closer and closer to them, until you are a foot away from an old man sitting on a garbage mound in Dumpville emptying tin cans into Shit Creek, or jump farther and farther away, until you can see how a certain place at 37.5 degrees latitude on the western edge of the North American continent was virtually impossible for fifteenth-century explorers to sail to. Zooming way in and zooming way out on a given place in a city—in this case, San Francisco—is just as intoxicating, just as great an intellectual adventure, as making the forty cosmic jumps in Boeke's book.

In fact, in one way, it's an even greater intellectual adventure. For cities are three-dimensional entities like the girl holding the cat, but they also exist in a fourth dimension: time. And so the explorer of San Francisco has the opportunity not only to, for example, learn about how many blocks long Joice Street is, and its spatial relation to Dashiell Hammett Street and Powell Street, and the little shrine to Saint Francis that sits on the west side of the first landing on the steps that run between Pine and California streets, but to learn about the jolly huntsman and notary who gave the street its name, and the Nob Hill wilderness he hunted in, and the murderer who was hanged because of that wilderness, and the vigilante movement that was involved in that hanging, and the seventeenth-century Spanish law against wearing capes that indirectly led to San Francisco being called San Francisco, and so on pretty much ad infinitum.

All of which is to say that cities are four-dimensional universes, and any given place within them is a portal that opens into an inconceivably rich treasure trove, one that exists in both the present and the past. In *Ulysses*, that unparalleled exploration of the universe of Dublin on a single day, James Joyce wrote, "Any object, intensely regarded, may be a gate of access to the incorruptible eon of the gods." With the "incorruptible eon of the gods" part taken down a couple of metaphysical notches, that line could be the guiding motto of this book. Or, putting it in a considerably less lofty way, the explorations here are basically variations on the six-degrees-of-separation theme: you can take just about any place in a city, and if you look at it from enough different angles, you'll be able to connect it to just about anything under the sun.

A word on the dual art-and-text nature of this book: I've always loved books about cities that include illustrations, and some of my favorite books about San Francisco have had memorable art. The first great book about the city, *The Annals of San Francisco*, published in 1855, boasted no fewer than 150 superb engravings. Charles Caldwell Dobie's 1933 book, *San Francisco: A Pageant*, was accompanied by dozens of fine pencil drawings by E. H. Suydam. Robert O'Brien's now forgotten but first-rate *This Is San Francisco* (1948) featured charming drawings by Antonio Sotomayor. Chiang Yee both wrote and illustrated his 1964 book, *The Silent Traveller* in San Francisco. And the dean of San Francisco's chroniclers, Herb Caen, teamed up with accomplished watercolorist Dong Kingman on the 1967 book *San Francisco: City on Golden Hills*.

The art in these books added an important and ineffable dimension to their portrayals of San Francisco and confirmed for me again the truth of Alice's Wonderland credo, "What is the use of a book without pictures?" (The full quote reads "pictures or conversation?" but since there is little or no conversation in this book, the quote has been truncated.) So when I had the opportunity to collaborate with the artist Paul Madonna on this book, I jumped at the chance.

I've been a huge fan of Paul's ever since I first saw *All Over Coffee*, his sui generis "comic strip"—more like exquisite passing glimpses of city life, accompanied by haiku-like texts—that ran for twelve years in the *San Francisco Chronicle*. I don't know any artist who captures San Francisco as precisely and evocatively as Paul. He's a spectacular draftsman, but that's not what sets his work apart. A North Beach artist I know put his finger on it: "His work is mysterious." Paul has a unique ability to summon up the shadow side of a city, the dark side of the urban moon. He's somehow able to evoke the simultaneous everydayness and grandeur of a cityscape, to uncover the sublime in the decrepit—and vice versa. He's a poet with pen and ink.

Paul and I began collaborating on a monthly feature in the *Nob Hill Gazette*, with a book in mind from the start. This project has been a full, equal, and extremely fun partnership between writer and artist. We went on field trips (some of them of borderline legality and safety) to find sites we felt needed to be included and afterward decided together what the final sixteen would be and what order they would go in. It would be as accurate to say that my text illustrates his drawings as to say that his drawings illustrate my text. Both elements are independent and stand on their own. And—we hope—they also illuminate each other.

We chose sites because we felt they worked visually and that I would have something interesting to say about them, and we wanted to include sites both famous and obscure, glamorous and gritty. If I had to compare my process of researching and selecting what to write about with anything, I'd say it was not unlike that engaged in by the narrator in Dylan Thomas's "A Child's Christmas in Wales," who plunges his hands into the snow at the edge of the carol-singing sea and brings out whatever stories he can find. If the ones I pulled out give both visitors and longtime residents some new, informative, and entertaining perspectives on the little universe that I love, San Francisco, I will be content.

"Any object, intensely regarded, may be a gate of access
to the incorruptible eon of the gods."
—JAMES JOYCE, *ULYSSES*

"San Francisco is a world to explore . . .
Have yourself an adventure in heaven, in the beautiful
and ugly heaven that is San Francisco."
—WILLIAM SAROYAN

CHAPTER 1

# JOICE STREET

## THREE UNIVERSES IN THREE BLOCKS

IN THE VAST library that is a city, every street is a different book. Some are like "see Jane run" primers, safe and sane; they start from an expected place and end up somewhere equally predictable. But others are as weird as Herman Melville's *Pierre* or Mikhail Bulgakov's *The Master and Margarita*. They may begin in a swanky neighborhood and end up in squalor, or go from being a soulless arterial to a dirt lane. One of the jarring joys of city streets, and cities in general, is precisely this narrative discontinuity. Unlike the natural world, cities are constantly contradicting themselves. They are filled with Potemkin facades, false climaxes, wrong turns, and bizarre transformations. And the shorter the distance in which the metamorphosis takes place, the more intoxicatingly Kafkaesque it is.

In San Francisco, the Gregor Samsa Award goes to . . . Joice Street. In just three blocks, this little street traverses three completely different urban universes. It starts as an unexpectedly grand stairway in the teeming heart of the city, ascends the glittering heights of Nob Hill, and then descends into the bedraggled depths of Chinatown.

The Joice Street steps run north off Pine Street just east of Powell. Most people just think of Pine as the fastest way to get out of downtown, but if you take your eye off the timed lights, you realize you are barreling through an open-air Museum of the Quintessential City, a time capsule that has preserved the American metropolis in its archetypal 1920s form.

What makes this part of town, and the adjoining Tenderloin, unique is its old apartment buildings. This approximately forty-acre area, bordered by Powell Street on the east and the Polk–Van Ness corridor on the west, boasts a greater concentration of four-to-eight-story apartment buildings and residential hotels, most built between 1907 and 1929, than any other city on the West Coast. In recognition of this, the Lower Nob Hill Apartment Hotel District was entered into the National Register of Historic Places in 1991. Technically, the only east–west streets in the historic area are Bush, Sutter, and Post, but the omission of Pine seems arbitrary: several addresses on it are included on the register's list of significant buildings, and it was developed at about the same time and in the same style.

And that style evokes city life in its purest form—dense, heterogeneous, atomistic, crowded, solitary, electric. The dozens of old apartments here, which run the gamut from elegant to decrepit, give Lower Nob Hill an intense, million-stories-in-the-Naked-City charm found nowhere else in this town.

Some of those stories were told by Dashiell Hammett, creator of the legendary San Francisco detective Sam Spade, whose footprints leave a ghostly trail all across this neighborhood. One of the most evocative of those trails starts a block south of the Joice Street steps, on tiny Burritt Alley, next to the Tunnel Top bar above the Stockton Tunnel. Here a plaque on the wall reads, "On approximately this spot Miles Archer, partner of Sam Spade, was done in by Brigid O'Shaughnessy." It's fitting that a city that takes its mythology as seriously as San Francisco does would put up a plaque that commemorates a fictional murder.

Moving from the fictional universe of *The Maltese Falcon* to that of Hammett's actual life in one hundred feet, the trail crosses Bush Street to Dashiell Hammett Street (formerly Monroe), where Hammett lived at No. 20 as a struggling young writer. It heads up this atmospheric little street to Pine Street, crosses that fast-moving throughway . . . and suddenly turns into a yellow brick road of marvel, the Joice Street steps.

An elegant set of steps is the last thing you'd expect to come upon in this dense neighborhood of corner stores and dry cleaners and apartments that have not changed since Sam Spade walked out their doors. Equally unexpected is the fact that they begin just downhill from the corner of Powell Street, the most storied of all the city's downtown streets, with its cable cars clattering down from the big hotels atop Nob Hill to Union Square. But walk halfway toward Stockton on Pine and there they are, the Joice Street steps, one of the hundreds of stairways of different lengths, materials, atmospheres, and destinations that provide delicious pedestrian slinkways, shortcuts for children of all ages, and metaphysical emergency exits all across San Francisco.

Halfway up the Joice Street steps is another unexpected time-out from urban reality: a tiny shrine to the city's patron saint and namesake, Saint Francis of Assisi. Compassionate, loving, a friend to animals and the poor, a radical and primitive Christian, Saint Francis is such a perfect fit with this city that it's easy to forget San Francisco might easily have been called San Ignacio. After all, it was Saint Ignatius of Loyola's Jesuit order that for a century established and ran the missions in Spain's New World colonies. It was only in 1767 that they were expelled from New Spain and replaced with the Franciscans—just two years before the Sacred Expedition that colonized California. (In one of the stranger episodes in Spanish history, the Jesuit expulsion was partially triggered by a "sumptuary law" that restricted men's wearing of voluminous capes and limited the breadth of their sombreros. This law was seen as "an insult to Castilian pride" and led to "hat and cloak riots" that caused King Carlos III to flee and played a role in his decision to suppress the Jesuits.) Since St. Ignatius was not exactly a poster child for the future cool, gray city of love—he was a driven former soldier whose followers were known as "God's marines"—this was apparently fortuitous for San Francisco's self-image, although former Jesuit seminarian and eternally recurring governor Jerry Brown would probably beg to differ. In fact, the Jesuits are the most liberal order within the Catholic Church, with a very San Francisco–like commitment to social justice, so San Ignacio would have been as appropriate a name as San Francisco.

The steps end soon after the shrine, but Joice Street continues to rise, past some apartment buildings whose ordinariness, on this urban byway so deep in the city's heart that every inch feels sanctified, is somehow satisfying, until it crests and slopes a few yards down to California Street. From Pine to California is only one block, but those few yards take you from an unromantic east–west roadway jammed with speeding cars to what was the city's grandest boulevard in the days when the nouveaux and old-veaux riches promenaded in their plebeian-enraging finery.

## THE FAVELAS OF FERN HILL

Nob Hill is famous the world over as a (no longer particularly accurate) byword for ostentatious wealth. But when the city was first settled, and for some years after that, it was more like a favela—high elevation, low tax bracket. Like all the city's hills in the early days, Fern Hill (its original name) was treeless, sandy, and windswept, and its eastern slope, the one California Street now runs down toward the Financial District, was so steep that it discouraged most people from walking up it, let alone building houses. A newspaper called it "a Sahara of desolation." A few houses were scattered around—the city's first elite residential neighborhood was on Stockton north of Washington—but not many. On top of the hill was a shantytown, where several families lived in huts made of salvaged material, as pigs, goats, ducks, and chickens ran around in a crude barnyard.

This favela pattern, in which poor people took up residence in the heights, characterized three of the city's downtown hills—Nob, Telegraph, and Russian—during the city's early history. The fourth, Rincon Hill, was the only upscale address at that time.

Nob Hill's remoteness and inaccessibility actually cost a luckless criminal his life. In 1851, a murderer named James Stuart was arrested near the hill's summit after a report of a different suspect was circulated. Stuart was well-dressed and well spoken and would probably have been released, but when his captors learned he had started from the Mission and was heading for the Plaza (Portsmouth Square), they decided to detain him. Only someone trying to avoid detection, they reasoned, would have taken such a difficult, steep route through the desolate sand dunes and scrub brush. Stuart was later hanged by the First Committee of Vigilance—a fate that more than one contemporary San Franciscan has probably wished upon out-of-town Uber drivers who are ordered by their GPS to take illogical, Stuart-like routes across town.

But Nob Hill, like all of early San Francisco, was a chaotic mixture of wilderness and civilization. The sandy wasteland where Stuart was arrested was within two or three blocks of a cluster of middle-class houses, which were actually located on Joice Street. In March 1850, an advertisement in the *Daily Alta California* announced that "the three 2-story dwellings on the corner of California and Joice streets, having a grand view of the harbor, etc.," were for rent for $100 a month each—no small sum of money.

There were a few fine houses on Nob Hill, most notably the Tillinghast house, a large, square building with verandas on all four sides at the corner of Pine and Mason. But the Clay Street Hill, as it was also known, did not become a desirable neighborhood until 1873. What brought the blue bloods up to Taylor and Jones and Clay streets was a new form of transportation, created by a young Scot who was inspired to build it after he witnessed a terrible accident at the base of the very hill he would tame.

## HALLIDIE'S FOLLY

The form of transportation that would become synonymous with San Francisco around the world had its genesis on a cold and rainy winter day in 1869. A team of horses was laboring hard to pull an overcrowded horsecar up the 8.3 percent grade on Jackson Street between Kearny and Stockton. As the team struggled up the hill, one of the horses slipped on the wet cobblestones. The car slid downhill, dragging the horses behind it, and came to rest at Kearny Street, where the mutilated horses lay in the intersection.

One of the horrified onlookers who rushed to help the horses was a young Scot named Andrew Hallidie. The incident left such a powerful impression on him that he determined to build a public transit system that would carry passengers up San Francisco's steep streets without subjecting horses to such "great cruelty and hardship."

(During the city's early years, the intersection of Jackson and Kearny was associated with a well-known and colorful character named Dan Curran. Because the grade of the hill was too steep for standard two-horse cars to climb, Curran was stationed at the corner of Kearny and Jackson with an extra horse, which he would hitch to the two-horse teams to assist them in pulling the car up the hill.

When Curran's horse reached the top, he would turn it loose to make its way to the bottom of the hill. According to Curran, the horse was virulently anti-Chinese and restrained himself from kicking out at the many Chinese in his vicinity only because he was working—an anecdote that doubtless says more about the ubiquitous anti-Chinese bigotry of the time than it does about Curran's horse's sentiments.)

Andrew Hallidie was one of those intrepid self-made immigrants who fill the pages of San Francisco's early history. He and his Scottish father—also an inventor and machinist—sailed from London to San Francisco in 1852 and headed for the gold fields. Like most Argonauts, they failed to strike it rich. But Hallidie, already a skilled engineer, began the kind of work that would eventually make him one of San Francisco's leading citizens. At the age of nineteen, he constructed a 220-foot-long wire suspension bridge over the American River. After various hair-raising adventures in the Mother Lode—he was snowed in for a month, buried in a six-hundred-foot tunnel, and swept downstream for half a mile after trying to break up a logjam in a river—he returned to San Francisco, where he opened a factory at Chestnut and Mason and began producing wire rope.

Wire rope was an essential part of the 1869–1870 Hallidie invention that made the cable car possible—the "Endless Ropeway," an aerial tramway that carried ore in large buckets from the mines to transportation depots. Hallidie realized he

could use the same concept in a street railroad system and began working on the project. But few believed he could pull it off. He wrote of "being laughed at for my pains, and the public refusing to have anything to do with the scheme." Locals derided it as "Hallidie's Folly."

But Hallidie persevered, overcoming technical problems, patent obstacles, bureaucratic roadblocks, and reluctant investors. He had to invest $20,000 of his own money and was able to secure a loan from his primary investor only by mortgaging his house. Finally, in 1873, the thirty-seven-year-old Hallidie was ready to test his invention.

## THE WIRE HOLDS

Just after midnight on August 2, 1873, Hallidie stood at the top of Clay Street, looking down into the foggy depths below and preparing to launch his cable car on its trial descent. The route he had chosen was daunting. From the summit at Jones Street, the line dropped six steep blocks to a lower terminus on Kearny, 307 vertical feet below. The line's total length was 2,800 feet; its steepest grade, between Jones and Taylor, was 16.24 percent. The cable on which the cars, and the lives of the passengers, depended was made up of six strands of nineteen wires each, with a tensile strength of 160,000 pounds per square inch. This "rope," about two thirds of an inch in diameter and 11,000 feet long, was connected by a mechanical grip to the bottom of an open-sided grip car, or "dummy," which in turn pulled a closed passenger car, or trailer. The system was powered by a steam plant at Clay and Leavenworth, a block away from the summit.

Hallidie was ready. But at the last moment his gripman, a retired locomotive engineer, lost his nerve and refused to go. So Hallidie, who had plunged down raging Sierra rivers and trusted the strength of his cable the way he trusted his breath, took his place. He seized the grip, released the brake, and the dummy (the trailer had been left off for this first run) began its inaugural descent down Nob Hill. It made it to the bottom safely, was turned around, transferred to the up line, and pulled smoothly back to the top.

"There was no frivolity," Hallidie recalled. "The whole affair was serious, and when it was done, there was simply a mutual handshaking, and nothing but cold water drank." Nor did any spectators cheer, for the simple reason that they were asleep. Only one observer commemorated the great occasion: an "enthusiastic Frenchman" in a building near Mason Street, who "thrust his red night-capped head out of the window as we went by on the down trip and threw us a faded bouquet."

On the first public ride that afternoon, the "revenue run"—a requirement of the franchise—the car was packed with men. But a young lady began following the car on foot. After more than a block, she was taken aboard by "male sympathizers." The nameless young woman walked up to the cash box and dropped in a five-cent piece, saying that for the rest of her life, she would have the satisfaction of knowing she was the first woman ever to ride a cable car.

Hallidie's invention opened up Nob Hill. Now that it was easy to get to the summit, San Francisco's blue bloods launched a mansion-building frenzy on Taylor, California, and other streets. The city's former tony neighborhoods, Rincon Hill and South Park, lost their cachet as the money headed to the northeast. The area around Joice Street went from being the windblown sticks to the most sought-after address in town. California Street, in particular, became an over-the-top architectural wealth display case, one crazily ornate Victorian popping up after the next.

But one thing did not change. At the eastern foot of Nob Hill, just two blocks from the grand mansions on Mason Street, stood San Francisco's poorest and most densely populated neighborhood, Chinatown. And then as now, Joice Street ran right through the no-man's-land between these parallel universes.

## THE SAINT OF SACRAMENTO STREET

California Street boasts its own cable car line, the successor of Hallidie's Clay Street route. The California line plies its straight, 1.4-mile east–west route between Van Ness and near the foot of Market Street. Joice crosses California just below Powell Street—the only corner in the city where the cable cars are controlled by a human operator, who sits in the little kiosk on the southeast corner. Elegant apartment buildings and the Twin's Armoire, an appropriately eccentric boutique once run by the queens of San Francisco eccentricity, the late, lamented Brown twins, provide a patrician flanking for Joice on the north side of California Street.

No sooner does this chameleonic little street cross California and head toward Sacramento Street, however, than it loses its summit-of-Nob-Hill glamour and descends into utilitarian edge-of-Chinatown drabness, contemptuously mooned by the unattractive derrieres of big buildings on both sides. This bleak stretch is worth braving, however, because at the end of this block, on the southeast corner of Joice and Sacramento, stands the Cameron House, which for four decades was the home and headquarters of one of the most remarkable women in the history of San Francisco.

The Cameron House is made of "clinker" bricks, ones discolored and twisted in the 1906 fire. It's appropriate that this building is made of material that survived a catastrophe. For the Cameron House protected countless Chinese girls and young women who had been forced into sex slavery in Chinatown.

Donaldina Cameron, after whom the building was named, was an indomitable Presbyterian missionary who dedicated her life to helping those unfortunates. Cameron arrived at the Presbyterian Mission Home in 1895, a naive twenty-five-year-old. She soon got her baptism of fire. She had been at the home for less than a month when the superintendent, Margaret Culbertson, received word that a young girl was being held as a sex slave on Bartlett Alley in Chinatown. She asked Cameron if she was sure she wanted to come with her on a rescue mission, warning her young charge that "this is a vile alley."

"Of course I want to help," Cameron replied.

Joined by a translator named Ah Cheng, the two women hurried down to Stockton Street, where two policemen armed with sledgehammers and axes joined them. They walked quickly to shadowy Bartlett Alley, where they found the brothel. Repeated poundings on the door yielded no response. Three more policemen were summoned. Two officers pried off a window grating and led Culbertson and Cameron into a room lit by a single candle. A girl was crouched miserably in a corner, her face filled with fear. Culbertson asked her if she wanted to go to the mission home. "I come! I come!" the girl said.

The officers tried the door, but it was locked. They smashed the lock open with a hammer. A Chinese man came running up, shouting, "Stop! Stop! You break my house!" He stared balefully at the girl, who cringed against Culbertson. "You!" he screamed. "May all your ancestors curse you, and turn you into a turtle!" The terrified girl hid her face.

The officers ordered the brothel keeper to open the street door or they would break it down. Still cursing, the man slid back the bolt. Culbertson, Cameron, and the police led the sobbing girl onto the street.

The practice of sex slavery in Chinatown was one of the darkest chapters in the city's history. For eighty years, Chinese traffickers kidnapped, tricked, or purchased girls and young women in China and brought them to San Francisco, where they were forced to work as prostitutes or as domestic servants (often de facto slaves) known as *mui tsai*. Hatchet-wielding "highbinders," the foot soldiers of criminal tongs, fought bloody battles to control the highly lucrative Chinatown vice rackets, which also included opium dens and gambling. The violence was so out of control that many residents of Chinatown fled.

Donaldina Cameron and her assistants, in particular her right-hand woman, a former household slave named Tien Fu Wu, played a decisive role in bringing this barbaric practice to an end. During her forty years of service, Cameron rescued thousands of girls and young women from slavery.

Cameron slept in a modest bedroom on the second floor of the building that is now named after her, and which still provides social services for the people of Chinatown. As you walk along Joice Street, you can still see the window of the room where one of the city's greatest heroes lived.

## ERASTUS JOICE,
## THE JOLLY SPORTSMAN OF NOB HILL

Joice Street was named for a typically resilient forty-niner who rejoiced (no pun intended) in the very nineteenth-century name Erastus Volney Joice. Born in New York in 1810, Joice became a Wall Street lawyer but declared bankruptcy in 1843. He appeared in San Francisco in January 1849, a comparatively venerable thirty-nine-year-old in a city dominated, then as now, by fortune seekers in their twenties. After being elected vice president at the first meeting of Democrats in the city and state, Joice began buying up real estate, including part of one of the instant city's first big hotels, the Union Hotel on Portsmouth Square (which he providentially sold just a month before it was destroyed by one of the six catastrophic fires that ravaged the Gold Rush city). He became a notary, living with his wife in "an odd looking little box of a place" at 807 Stockton near Clay, a block south of the town's first fashionable neighborhood. Strangely, although Joice Street was named after him, he did not live on it.

Erastus V. Joice would have simply gone down in history as a notary with a Dickensian name and a good eye for real estate, had he not come to genial life in one of the most charming reminiscences written about Gold Rush San Francisco, *Men and Memories of San Francisco in the "Spring of '50"* by T. A. Barry and B. A. Patten, keepers of a popular eponymous saloon at 116 Montgomery Street. They wrote, "Mr. Joice is, and has been for many years, a notary, and bids fair to live a half century longer, if one may judge by his step and manner on California Street;

and better still, by the ground he will get over, and the steep hill-sides he can climb, in a day's shooting, coming in full of spirit and fun, when some of the boys are lame and disagreeably quiet. We hope he may bag his game for many years to come, for we do certainly like good-natured men."

In an odd bit of street-name trivia, only the first of Joice's blocks, between Pine and California, was originally named after the happy hunter. The block between California and Sacramento was called Buena Vista, and the one between Sacramento and Clay was called Prospect Place. Considering the quantum urban jumps Joice makes in its three blocks, the fact that it once could not stick with the same name for more than one of them seems singularly appropriate.

## CHAPTER 2

# PIER 24

## PORT CITY

TODAY, SAN FRANCISCO'S Embarcadero is a magnificent promenade. The two-mile stretch between Oracle Park and Pier 39, which passes under the mighty Bay Bridge and past a procession of grand gray finger piers, with the ever-changing spectacle of the bay as a backdrop, is one of the great waterfront strolls in the world.

But it is impossible to walk along this clean, peaceful, parklike waterfront without regretting the loss of the old, dirty, noisy, smelly, chaotic, dangerous one.

The City Front, as the Embarcadero used to be called when it was the city's front door, was not glamorous. In fact, much of it was downright ugly—except at night, when it became ineffably romantic. But it was real. It was a working port. For more than a century, to walk from, say, the mouth of Mission Creek to the piers at the foot of Telegraph Hill, was to witness the humming and grinding and gearshifting of a vast, intricate, glorious, rusty machine.

Take the year 1933. In the darkest depths of the Depression, seven thousand ships pulled into and out of the city's eighty-two piers. Weather-beaten vessels from Liberia and Japan and New York loaded and unloaded their cargo. State Belt Line trains hissed and clanged and crashed next to the piers. Winches and cranes performed their intricate ballet. Smells of copra (dried coconut meat) and coffee and sugar and rotting piers and mud drifted past the Ferry Building as thousands of truck drivers and sailors and shipping-line executives and office workers and longshoremen poured in and out of the city.

Of all the people who swarmed over the waterfront, the ones most essential to its functioning were longshoremen. Before the late 1950s, when container ships and high-powered cranes revolutionized the industry (and spelled doom for the city's working waterfront), San Francisco was predominantly a "break-bulk" port, meaning most of the cargo it handled was shipped in pieces—bags, sacks, boxes—capable of being handled by one man or a few men. Those men were longshoremen—practitioners of a job as old as the first seaport.

It was not a job for the faint of heart or weak of back. A 1932 Bureau of Labor Statistics bulletin describes some of the cargo that men or gangs of men were expected to lift. They ranged from bags of flour (100 to 150 pounds) to coffee (135 to 200 pounds) to bales of Egyptian cotton (750 pounds) to hogsheads of tobacco (500 to 1,000 pounds). Manhandling this cargo was difficult and dangerous. The cafés and saloons along the City Front were filled with men missing fingers and limbs and eyes or permanently bent over from years of intense physical strain. Many men lost their lives.

In its heyday, the port handled almost every type of cargo imaginable, from states across the country and countries all over the world, including, according to a 1926 report, "canned fruits and vegetables, dried fruits, cotton, leather, autos, minerals, coffee, sugar, copra, tea, fibers, tin, nitrates, peanuts, crab meat, gunnies, manufactured machinery and general merchandise and other articles too numerous to relate."

And, of course, there was human cargo. The port handled passenger craft of all kinds, from bay ferries, riverboats, and coastwise steamers to big oceangoing liners. Alongside sweating stevedores and truck drivers and clerks tallying cargo being unloaded, taxis delivered well-dressed men and women in dresses, who walked up gangplanks to luxury liners with destinations all over the globe. In a typical month in 1948, passenger and cargo ships departed from San Francisco for the British Isles, Italy, Germany, Holland, Belgium, Sweden, Canada, both coasts of South America, the Caribbean, India, Pakistan, Hong Kong, Japan, Indonesia, Australia, New Zealand, the Philippines, and the Dutch East Indies. In that year, more than 150 shippers and agents were working in the city.

The port permeated every aspect of city life: as late as 1961, it supported the livelihood of one third of every San Franciscan. But its significance went beyond the economic.

The port was a city symphony, a universe unto itself, an endlessly fascinating spectacle at water's edge, with its own rhythms and moving parts and secrets. And it was the last link with a great maritime thread that ran through the city's entire history, from the great age of exploration when California was an unknown spot on maps, the blanks filled in over the centuries by men braving alien seas, to the first Spanish vessel to sail through the Golden Gate, to the ships that brought the forty-niners. As long as the port was functioning, San Francisco was not just a city built on the water: it belonged to it.

## THE PIERS

The most notable survivors of the port's glory days, besides the Ferry Building, are its piers. About two dozen finger piers, most of them extending about eight hundred feet into the bay, are lined up on both sides of the Ferry Building. The piers have three components: their substructures and pilings, their transit sheds (long buildings constructed atop the piers), and, most visibly, their bulkhead buildings, with their elegant decorated fronts. It's these bulkhead buildings, or pier ends, that most powerfully evoke San Francisco's *On the Waterfront* days.

The city's waterfront did not start out looking like this. As Michael Corbett writes in *Port City: The History and Transformation of the Port of San Francisco 1848–2010*, until the end of the nineteenth century, these shed fronts were cheap

and ugly. Wooden piers deteriorated so quickly that it made no sense to spend money on their appearance. But the invention of concrete-clad piles in 1901 and reinforced concrete in 1908 justified the expense of an ornamental facade.

Starting in 1912, inspired by the City Beautiful movement, with its belief in grand, classically inspired public buildings and spaces, port authorities redid the piers north of the Ferry Building in a neoclassic style (modeled after New York City's Chelsea Piers) and chose a Mission Revival style for the piers to the south.

Pier 26, the building on the right in the drawing (it stands directly under the Bay Bridge), was built in 1912–1913 in Mission Revival style. The Pier 24 Annex, pictured on the left, was built in 1928 on the connecting wharves between Pier 24 and Pier 26. (Pier 24, built in 1915 also in Mission Revival style, burned down in 1997.) Like many of the piers and other structures on the waterfront, the Pier 24 Annex has been rehabilitated and now serves a completely different function: it houses a world-class photography gallery, which is free and can be viewed only by appointment.

In an intriguing architectural footnote, the Mission Revival style connects the piers south of the Ferry Building with the most powerful, and for decades widely hated, corporate entity in the history of California. As Corbett notes, the Southern Pacific Railroad, aka the Octopus, constructed many of its buildings in

that style in an attempt to evoke California's romantic Spanish past. (Southern Pacific used *Sunset* magazine, which it began publishing in 1898, for similar promotional purposes.) As it happened, before the State Belt Railroad began serving the areas both north and south of the Ferry Building, Southern Pacific was the only railroad serving the area to its south. As Corbett writes, "Whether it was intentional or not, the use of architectural imagery associated with the Southern Pacific in an area it had long served exclusively may have reinforced the connection between the southern part of the port and the railroad." It's fascinating, if a bit deflating, to think that the *Ramona*-esque architectural style of the piers south of the Ferry Building may have been an early example of corporate branding.

These mighty pier ends give the waterfront a unique air of industrial gravitas. Especially north of the Ferry Building, they form a muscular and elegant wall, whose long history only adds to their mystique. And it turns out that those piers, and other surviving features of the old waterfront, are unique. San Francisco's working port may be only a shadow of what it once was, but more of its historic heart has survived than in any other American city. As Corbett writes, "Despite the loss of many of its piers and changes in its setting, San Francisco alone retains, in addition to its seawall and bulkhead wharf, rows of piers and a diversity of other structures—car-ferry slips, restaurants for workers, pile-driving rigs, the Ferry Building—that convey the scale and significance of the ports of the early 20th century."

## THE NELSON STEAMSHIP COMPANY

Because San Francisco Bay connects with both the ocean and inland waterways, the port of San Francisco was used by ships plying every imaginable route. Until the Bay Bridge was built, tens of thousands of people used ferries to commute into the city every day, and ocean liners carried passengers to Europe and Asia. But few people realize that San Francisco was also the home of a large coastwise fleet, which plied the Pacific coast between San Diego and the ports of the Pacific Northwest.

One of the leading coastwise lines was the Nelson Steamship Company. Between 1922 and 1936, it was the principal tenant of Pier 24.

The cover of Corbett's *Port City* features a photograph, taken between 1930 and 1935, that captures Pier 24 in action. A large sign over the pier's arch, below the Mission-style facade of the bulkhead building, bears the words "Nelson Steamship

Company." Two freighters are berthed on the north side of the pier. A State Belt Line locomotive, belching smoke, is halfway out of the bulkhead building and halfway across the sidewalk, presumably pulling railcars loaded with lumber or other cargo from the freighters. A few pedestrians wait for the train to cross to the west side of the Embarcadero, where the tracks run. There are no warning signals and there is no crossing guard.

The story of the Nelson Steamship Company, one of the oldest American shipping companies, has all the classic elements of a San Francisco business story during the Gold Rush era: a poor but hardworking immigrant, failure in the mines, an adroit pivot to other enterprises, a devastating setback caused by a financial scandal in the city, recovery followed by a brilliant business move, great success and wealth, and finally bankruptcy—the latter, mercifully, happening long after the company's founder had gone to his final reward.

That founder, Charles Nelson, was born in Denmark in 1830. He went to sea at age thirteen, earning the princely sum of seventy-five cents a month. Nelson learned to do everything on a ship—he even served as the cook—and rose to become mate. After making a voyage to New York, Nelson sailed home in 1849, having promised his mother he would return five years after he left. It was the last time he would see his parents: his father died in 1850, his mother in 1863.

Heeding the siren song of gold, Nelson sailed to San Francisco in 1850. He didn't do very well at mining, but he bought a whaling boat, which he and a comrade loaded with freight and passengers and, in an impressive feat of oarsmanship and perseverance, rowed ninety miles upriver from Sacramento to Marysville. He continued to ferry passengers and cargo on this route in the whaling boat, making extra money by buying vegetables in Marysville and selling them in Sacramento. Nelson took the money he saved and deposited it in the Adams Express Company bank in San Francisco, intending to use it to repair the whaler. But a financial crisis known as the Panic of 1855 led to a run on the Adams bank that drove it and other leading San Francisco banks out of business, and Nelson lost all his money. (Adams's loss was Wells Fargo's gain: the more conservatively run bank picked up its bankrupt rivals' customers and became one of the leading banks in the West.)

Undaunted, the twenty-five-year-old Nelson continued his shipping operations and invested in a barkentine, the first one ever built on the Pacific coast. Then he made the moves that were to make his fortune. First, he purchased an interest in a lumber company that had large holdings in Humboldt County and

upgraded its lumber operations. Second—this was the masterstroke—he bought a line of tugboats, which he used to transport the lumber up and down the Pacific coast. As the profits rolled in, Captain Nelson, as he was now known, began investing in larger ships. Soon he opened his own lumber shipping company, the Charles Nelson Company.

Nelson became a pillar of the community. He was a four-time head of the San Francisco Chamber of Commerce, a founder of the Scandinavian Evangelical Lutheran Church, and a trustee of Mills College. He was well-read, had a direct and engaging manner, and was universally respected.

The lives of self-made nineteenth-century men such as Nelson inspire admiration, and their success may inspire envy. But there was one dark aspect of human existence that neither they nor anyone else at the time could control. Nelson and his first wife, Metha, also a Dane, had six children. All but one of them died in infancy.

After Metha died in 1896, Nelson married another Danish woman named Helen. They lived in a beautiful house with ten acres of well-kept grounds on Seminary Avenue in Oakland. Captain Nelson died in 1909.

The Nelson Steamship Company, incorporated in 1922 as a subsidiary of Nelson's lumber company, owned eighteen steamers, which plied both coastwise and intercoastal waters. Its coastwise cargo ships carried rice, coffee, petroleum, petroleum products, roofing products, salt, sugar, and canned goods on the run from San Francisco to the Northwest; in the opposite direction they carried lumber, canned goods, cereal products, manufactured steel products, and potatoes.

The shipping news in the March 28, 1913, edition of the San Francisco newspaper the *Call* lists the eleven thirty A.M. arrival of the Nelson Steamship Company steamer *North Fork*, twenty-three hours from Eureka, carrying 350,000 board feet of lumber. This is enough lumber to build twenty-eight two-thousand-square-foot homes. Since hundreds, probably thousands, of Nelson ships carried lumber to San Francisco over the decades, it is reasonable to assume that the equivalent of entire neighborhoods in the city were built with lumber carried on Charles Nelson ships and delivered to Pier 24.

## ANCHORS AWEIGH FOR LOS ANGELES

The Nelson Steamship Company was mostly a cargo operation, but it did own one passenger steamer, the *Nome City*, which ran regularly between San Francisco and the Pacific Northwest. The *Nome City* was part of a now forgotten coastwise passenger fleet that for two decades allowed travelers to cruise in comfort and style to ports up and down the Pacific coast, at prices and speeds that rivaled trains.

As Giles Brown writes in "The Culmination and Decline of Pacific Northwest Shipping, 1916–1936," an article that appeared in the July 1949 issue of the *Pacific Northwest Quarterly*, the Admiral Line enjoyed a virtual monopoly on coastwise shipping before World War I. But its two fastest ships, the *Harvard* and the *Yale*, were requisitioned by the U.S. government during the war, and after the war a rival line called LASSCO purchased them. They could make the trip from San Francisco to Los Angeles in eighteen hours, while Admiral's slow ships took twenty-five hours.

In response, the head of the Admiral Line, H. F. Alexander, tried to acquire two even faster requisitioned liners, the *Northern Pacific* and the *Great Northern*, the latter of which was being used as the flagship of the U.S. fleet. (The *Great Northern* had made her first Astoria, Oregon–San Francisco run for the 1915 Panama-Pacific International Exposition, arriving at the Greenwich Street wharf in San Francisco after a twenty-three-hour voyage.) The *Northern Pacific* burned at sea, but after shady negotiations with the Warren Harding administration (the vessel was sold to Admiral five days before bids were to be opened), Alexander acquired the *Great Northern*. The suspicious circumstances of the sale led to a congressional investigation, but no action was taken.

H. F. Alexander's new ship was brought through the new Panama Canal to San Francisco. Immodestly renamed the *H. F. Alexander*, she could sail from San Francisco to Los Angeles in just sixteen hours, a speed rivaling that of all but the fastest trains. Moreover, she set the standard for luxury for coastwise ships.

Admiral added two other large vessels to its fleet, the *Ruth Alexander* and the *Emma Alexander*. (Eighteen-year-old Thomas Fleming, who was to start San Francisco's leading African American newspaper, the *Sun-Reporter*, worked on the *Emma Alexander* for a summer as a bellboy—the only maritime job open to blacks at the time.) Admiral's coastwise fleet was wildly successful: between 1921 and 1926, its total annual passenger miles soared from forty-seven million to eighty-three million. The *H. F. Alexander* was so fast and made so many trips that one magazine claimed that she "probably has logged a greater mileage . . . than any vessel during a like period in the history of world commerce." Alexander was extolled as a maritime genius; at a luncheon, a judge gushed that the Admiral Line story "was one of the romances of the age."

Admiral offered its passengers first-class service. Both berth and meals were included in the fare, which was usually lower than rail fare. In a forerunner of future cruise ship pig-outs, the line invited passengers to eat all they wished from a buffet that often included six meat dishes. A free dance orchestra played after dinner. The one problem that Admiral could not resolve was seasickness. Faced with pleas from executives for ships that would not roll, marine engineers retorted that moderate rolling helped prevent capsizing. One expert said, "A live passenger is worth several dead ones, even if he were fractionally more seasick than the comfortably drowned ones," an opinion that probably was not used in Admiral's advertising campaigns.

But Admiral soon faced stiff competition, from LASSCO and Nelson as well as the McCormick Steamship Company, which had incorporated in 1923 and like Nelson had originated as a lumber company. (A McCormick ship carrying lumber off San Pedro had the unwelcome distinction of being torpedoed by a Japanese submarine on Christmas Day, 1941.) In 1928, Nelson boasted that it had the largest coastwise fleet, although most of its ships were slow and made of wood.

In 1925, Admiral was still riding high, easily raising $8.5 million in new capital. But the next decade would send it and the entire coastwise shipping trade to Davy Jones's locker.

A number of factors doomed the coastal lines. Rate wars, started by small shipping companies, inflicted the first blow. Profits sank even as shipping tonnage increased. In 1929, the stock market crash weakened the industry, taking a particularly heavy toll on lines such as Nelson that were heavily invested in the lumber industry. The phenomenal rise of the automobile after World War I, and the growth of the trucking industry, further eroded shipping's prominence. And railroads continued to improve. In 1927, Southern Pacific opened its faster Cascade Line between California and the Northwest. It had always been cheaper to ship freight by sea than by rail, but when the Interstate Commerce Commission ruled in 1931 that railroads could reduce freight charges, the difference in cost was practically wiped out. The shipping lines were also hurt by the successful 1934 longshoremen's strike, which increased operating costs when revenue was drastically declining. And public confidence was damaged by shipwrecks along the coast, the horrors of which were played up by the press. When the *San Juan* sank in a collision off California in 1919, a paper printed twelve pictures of the disaster, one bearing the lurid caption "When Grinding Timbers and Rending Iron Sang Dirge of Sixty-Eight."

These multiple factors were too much to overcome. In 1936, Admiral, Nelson, and all the other coastwise shipping lines ended their passenger service. It's still possible to take a cruise from San Francisco to Los Angeles. But the era when you could board a fast, inexpensive luxury liner on the Embarcadero at six P.M., have a cocktail at sunset while looking at the Pacific Ocean, eat an excellent dinner, dance to a fine orchestra, enjoy a comfortable night's sleep in a private berth, and arrive in Los Angeles at ten A.M. the next morning has vanished as permanently as the Manila galleon that plied the same route five hundred years ago.

## CHAPTER 3

# DIVISION STREET

## UNHAPPY VALLEY

No NEIGHBORHOOD IN San Francisco has changed as rapidly and radically as South of Market. Until the 1990s, this most famous of the city's working-class neighborhoods was mostly still a grimy, semi-industrial area, its unlovely one-way arterials lined with auto repair shops, gas stations, and leather bars, its side streets and alleys filled with decaying old tenements. But starting with the first tech boom, and then moving into warp speed with the current one, most of South of Market has received the massive money makeover that has Botoxed out so many of San Francisco's wrinkles. Where boardinghouses and pawnshops once huddled, gleaming glass monoliths now reach arrogantly for the virtual sky, like so many Towers of Algorithmic Babel.

South of Market has been associated with poor and homeless men ever since the Gold Rush. When the world rushed in to San Francisco in 1849, at least half of the South of Market area—whose boundaries are Market Street on the north, the Embarcadero on the east, Mission Creek, King Street, and Division Street on the south, and roughly Eleventh Street on the west—either was submerged under the shallow waters of Mission Bay or was swampy wetlands. The instant city grew up around Yerba Buena Cove, which curved into what is now the Financial District as far as Montgomery Street. Thousands of men pitched tents in an area around the present-day Palace Hotel called Happy Valley. With the exception of two or three Yelamu Indian sites, this was the original settlement in South of Market.

Happy Valley was not an accurate name. Because the city had few springs and limited sources of drinking water, many of the inhabitants of the tent city resorted to digging shallow wells in the sandy soil. The water they drank was contaminated with human and animal waste, and the resulting dysentery was responsible for as many as five to ten deaths a day. Happy Valley was a miserable place, filled with sick and dying men.

The Happy Valley tent city soon disappeared and manufacturing moved in, setting South of Market on the blue-collar course it would follow for more than 150 years. Iron foundries, gasworks, blacksmith shops, shipbuilders, shot factories, and sawmills proliferated. The clay banks of Mission Creek, which entered Mission Bay near the location depicted here, attracted brick makers. Shipsmiths, stevedores, machinists, blacksmiths, boatmen, and other workingmen moved into the area, close to their jobs and where rents were cheaper.

In his short story "South of the Slot," Jack London wrote, "Old San Francisco . . . was divided by the Slot . . . North of the Slot were the theaters, hotels and shopping district, the banks and the staid, respectable business houses. South of the Slot were the factories, slums, laundries, machine shops, boiler works, and the abodes of the working class." For London, who was born in 1876 at Third and Brannan near South Park, being born South of the Slot (the cable car slot

that once ran down Market Street) was as great a badge of honor as being a true Cockney, born within the sound of Bow Bells. Well into the twentieth century, prizefights between South of Market boys and their rivals from North Beach and the Mission galvanized the entire neighborhood.

During the city's early years, two South of Market enclaves were aristocratic exceptions to the area's working-class character: South Park and Rincon Hill. South Park (see page 165) was a private oval with large mansions, designed after London's Berkeley Square; Rincon Hill afforded beautiful views of the bay. But these patrician outposts lasted for only a few decades. After the cable cars began rolling, South of Market's handful of wealthy residents moved to Nob Hill and later to Pacific Heights.

South of Market became even more deeply blue-collar after 1870. Large numbers of Irish, English, and German immigrants flooded in, moving into small apartments and rooming houses on Howard, Folsom, and Harrison and smaller side streets such as Clara, Clementina, Minna, and Russ. A significant Greek colony sprang up around Fourth and Folsom. One third of the city's boardinghouses and half its hotels and lodging houses were located there. The fact that one third of the city's restaurants were found there further demonstrated how many single men lived in the neighborhood.

But the most intriguing, and little-known, South of Market group was hoboes. These itinerant seasonal workers—fruit pickers, loggers, miners, or other casual laborers—flooded into the neighborhood's cheap flophouses during the winter months, then headed out of town in the spring. After the turn of the century, hoboes made up an increasing percentage of the neighborhood's population. In fact, the area around Third and Howard became a kind of hobo city within a city.

## FROM HOBOHEMIA TO SKID ROW

The first three decades of the twentieth century were the heyday of the American hobo. Because of its cheap hotels, employment agencies, and lax morals, San Francisco was the most popular city on the West Coast for these rootless, casual workers. From around 1905 until the Great Depression, the area around Fourth and Howard streets became what sociologist and former hobo Nels Anderson called a "hobohemia"—a ragged but thriving community that served the economic and social needs of hoboes.

Among the institutions that made up hobohemia were a plentiful supply of cheap hotels and lodging houses, whose proprietors would often serve as informal banks, watching their boarders' money so that they would not spend it all on a spree. (Hoboes typically came into town with only a $30 stake to last the winter.) Saloons offered cheap drinks and all-you-can-eat lunches for ten or fifteen cents and also sometimes served as informal employment agencies. Employment agencies would line up out-of-town work. Pawnshops on Third Street, lower Market, and the Embarcadero would accept a tool or item of clothing so that men who had run through their winter stake could buy a meal or rent a room. Wood yards operated by the Salvation Army and other charities gave needy men the chance to earn a day's food and a night's lodging by chopping wood for an hour or two. Pool halls and gambling joints offered entertainment, as did a cluster of Greek coffeehouses, featuring female Greek dancers, near Folsom Street. No fewer than fifty-one secondhand stores—including twenty-one in 1920 on the single block of Howard between Third and Fourth—offered cheap clothing.

But hoboes, and the neighborhood that supported them, were about to disappear from the American scene. Mechanization in logging, mining, and agriculture, as well as changes in workforce policies, decreased the need for migrant labor. When the Great Depression hit, these already precariously employed men lost their grip on even irregular employment. Hobohemia degenerated into a skid row. One evening in 1935, an observer witnessed fifteen hundred middle-aged and older men on Howard Street, many drunk, some passed out in the streets. Police and social workers said that drunkenness in the neighborhood had gotten much worse and its character had changed; while before it was happy drinking, now "it seemed to be the drinking of misery and despair."

By the late 1950s and early 1960s, skid row had expanded to Sixth Street and the Tenderloin, and the area around Fourth and Howard had become the haunt of old, poor men, many of them minorities, retired, and disabled. This final holdout was destroyed in the late 1960s and early 1970s, when the Yerba Buena Center for the Arts was built. San Francisco's hobohemia had jumped its last train.

## DUMPVILLE

The tech boom has transformed South of Market, but one street has remained untouched: Division. That functional, off-the-grid-and-under-the-freeway street, depicted here, is simply too shadowy, grimy, and downright ugly to attract much more than big-box stores and homeless people.

Division follows a former streambed of the old Mission Creek, a twisting waterway that once started in the Mission and emptied into Mission Bay. (For a short time during the Gold Rush, there was actually a rowboat service that took passengers from Mission Bay to Mission Dolores.) Thanks to that sinuous stream, in the late 1860s, the area around Division became home to one of the strangest communities in the history of San Francisco: Dumpville.

Dumpville was a scavenger colony, located, naturally, on top of San Francisco's main garbage dump. It started at Sixth and Channel and gradually expanded west and south until it covered more than twenty acres. For more than twenty years, Dumpville's population of 150 older men, most of them Italian, eked out a precarious livelihood under the control of a "dump trust" of six men. Dumpville featured a very early version of a recycling center. Residents, who lived in favela-like shanties, collected broken glass to sell to merchants in Chinatown, who would send it back to China, and smelted tin cans in a "quaint hut" surrounded by a ten-foot pile of cans.

It was not a bucolic existence. Mission Creek was so viscous and vile smelling it was called Shit Creek. Nonetheless, Dumpville remained in existence until 1895, when the authorities tore down its shanties.

Today, just two links with that vanished era remain. There's truncated Mission Creek, which dead-ends into a culvert just east of Seventh Street. And there are still homeless people on Division Street.

CHAPTER 4

# THE TIAN HOU TEMPLE

## THE SEA GODDESS

THE TIAN HOU Temple is Chinatown ground zero. It's on the most picturesque block of one of the quarter's most historic streets, Waverly Place. And while the hatchet men and courtesans who made Waverly infamous are long gone, the Tian Hou Temple remains, a living link with the faith that sustained the earliest Chinese immigrants.

The Tian Hou Temple is the oldest extant Taoist temple in the neighborhood and one of the oldest in the United States. The temple was originally built in 1852 in a different Chinatown location. That building, like everything else in the quarter, was destroyed in the 1906 earthquake. The church was rebuilt in 1910 in its current location at 125 Waverly Place, closed in 1955, and reopened in 1975. Since then it has been both a functioning Taoist temple and a major tourist attraction. So many tour groups trudge up the three dingy flights of stairs to gawk at the temple's interior that its keepers have festooned its walls with signs telling visitors how to behave.

Taoism was by far the most popular religion among nineteenth-century Chinese immigrants to California. It is an easy religion for Westerners to misunderstand, in part because many of its deities were once human beings and

consequently are often wrongly regarded as equivalent to Western saints. In fact, as Chuimei Ho and Bennet Bronson point out in *Three Chinese Temples in California: Marysville, Oroville, Weaverville*, these revered figures are actual deities who "can confer blessings directly, not indirectly like a Christian saint who has to intercede with a higher being. If you pray to Tian Hou, the Queen of Heaven, for a son or for safety during a storm, she is the one who confers or withholds those blessings."

Another easily misunderstood thing about Taoism, whose central tenet is living in harmony with the Tao, or "the Way," is its relaxed attitude toward doctrine. It is open to other spiritual practices. Like many other Taoist temples in California, the Tian Hou Temple not only contains dozens of figures of Taoist deities but also has a shrine dedicated to the Buddha and a statue of Guan Yin, the beloved Buddhist goddess of mercy. But according to Ho and Bronson, this does not mean it is both a Taoist and a Buddhist temple, simply that Taoism is a "rather mixed religion."

Among Chinese immigrants to California, the most popular deities were Guan Di, the god of war and brotherhood; Bei Di, the god of the north, known to martial artists as "Dark Warrior"; the aforementioned Guan Yin, a bodhisattva (one who has attained enlightenment but refuses to enter nirvana out of compassion

for suffering beings); and Tian Hou, also called Mazu, the "Empress of Heaven." In her earthly form, Tian Hou was a tenth-century shaman named Lin Moniang. Little is known about the historical Lin Moniang, but according to legend she saved members of her family from drowning, which is why she is worshipped as the sea goddess. Naturally, Chinese immigrants braving the Pacific to seek their fortunes in California prayed to Tian Hou. For the nineteenth-century Chinese in California she was a crucial deity, second in importance only to Guan Di.

## THE SHRINE

The heart of the Tian Hou Temple is its shrine to the eponymous goddess, but to get there you must first navigate through the religious equivalent of Dickens's *Old Curiosity Shop*. The single-room temple's small, opulent interior is so packed with figures of all sizes—whether they are deities, saints, or wise men is not immediately apparent—bells, carved reliefs with battle scenes, hanging ribbons, and various other objects that it is utterly baffling to the outside observer. However, there are invariably two or three elderly Chinese ladies engaged in various tasks in the temple, and some of them are happy to tell what they know about the temple. A friendly old woman named Susan served as an informal docent on a recent visit.

When you enter the temple, the first thing that you see is a big, intricately carved gilt wooden screen overhead on the wall in front of you. Susan explained that this screen has nothing to do with religion but is a historical scene depicting rulers and warriors from several different dynasties. Beyond the screen are ten or so carved female figures holding babies. These figures protected babies in the days of bad doctors, she said.

Near those figures is the most historically significant item in the temple, a bell. "They ring this at the opening of the temple," Susan said. According to Bennet and Ho, this bell, which dates to 1874, is the oldest temple bell in the United States. It was made for a now vanished Three Gods Shrine.

Next to the bell is a drum. As Bennet and Ho note, "Bells and drums in a Chinese temple are not musical instruments. Instead they are part of a communication system. The purpose is to call the gods' attention to an offering . . . Worshipers either sound the bell and drum themselves or, more often, let the temple keeper do it." Most nineteenth-century temple bells in the United States were cast in Foshan in the Pearl River Delta, a region known for the quality of its iron products.

The shrine to Tian Hou is in the center of the rear wall. In front of it, heaped with oranges and incense, is a fantastical carved rampaging lionlike creature, surrounded by figures representing the sun and the moon—this is to bring fertility, according to Susan.

The big central shrine, which is roped off, features a statue of Tian Hou herself. There are temple guardians on either side of her, as well as smaller statues of the goddess. Susan said they used to take these figures out onto the street during parades, but they don't do it anymore. To the left of Tian Hou's shrine is a glass case filled with sixty or so "horoscopes," as she called them, small figures of wise old men in different costumes, each one representing several different years.

Hanging overhead from little lanterns are hundreds of red strips of cloth with writing on them. Each is a prayer from an individual or organization that also donated cash to the temple. One is from an auto body shop in the South Bay. "Many people still come in and worship here, especially at Chinese New Year," Susan said.

Like so many things in Chinatown, the Tian Hou Temple is simultaneously touristy, run-down, and real. Beyond the tour groups, confusing profusion of deities, and handwritten signs forbidding photography and asking for donations, in this small, third-floor room in the heart of Chinatown you can still feel the faith that animated the immigrants who came here during the Gold Rush, and that still draws people here today.

## THE STREET WITH SEVEN NAMES

The balcony of the Tian Hou Temple offers an unexpected and spectacular view of Chinatown and parts of North Beach, including Coit Tower. It also overlooks one of the oldest and most fascinating streets in the city, Waverly Place—a two-block-long street that has had no fewer than seven names and nicknames. Originally called Calle de las Rosas, it was called Pike Street before 1861, when its name was changed for good to Waverly Place. The Cantonese name for the street means Tian Hou Temple Street, and the Chinese also called it *ho boon gai*, or "15 Cent Street," because that was the price of a haircut in one of the many barbershops that lined it. It was also known as the "Street of Slaves."

Initially, Pike Street appears to have been at least somewhat respectable. The city's first post office was located on the corner of Pike and Clay, and the street also featured a French restaurant called Raphael's as well as a coffeehouse started by the founder of Woodward's Gardens. But it soon became infamous both for its brothels and for violence. According to Richard Dillon in *Hatchet Men: The Story of the Tong Wars in San Francisco's Chinatown*, the first sex-related arrest on Pike was of an unlucky john named Antonio Juan Baptiste, who was fined $20 for visiting an establishment there. In *The Madams of San Francisco*, Curt Gentry writes that Pike Street was noted for having some of the early city's most luxurious brothels, as well as some of its seediest cribs. (A "crib" was a small room with almost nothing in it except a bed.) During the Gold Rush years, the whore-houses of San Francisco's two most famous and beautiful madams—one white, one Chinese—stood directly opposite each other on Pike. The first of these celebrated ladies of easy virtue was Belle Cora, reputed to be the best-dressed woman in San Francisco. Her presence at a play in late 1855, and the homicide that resulted from it, was one of the principal causes of the Second Committee of Vigilance—the largest vigilante movement in American history. The second fabled courtesan, Ah Toy, was one of the few Chinese prostitutes who worked her trade voluntarily. Ah Toy was not only stunningly beautiful, she was a shrewd and self-confident woman who soon graduated to becoming a madam and used the courts to demand her rights. She retired after about ten years in the business, married a wealthy Chinese man, and moved to San Jose. After his death, she sold

clams in Alviso. Most Chinese prostitutes died before they were thirty; Ah Toy lived to be almost one hundred.

During the 1850s, brawls, stabbings, and shootings became regular occurrences on Pike, the most disreputable part of which was known as Cat Alley (name number seven). Its descent into squalor was why its name was changed to Waverly. According to historian Albert Shumate, Pike Street was given to the city by Dr. Augustus J. Bowie, "whose property and house were situated in that block in the early 1850s. It was named in honor of his wife, a member of a well known Maryland family. When the street became notorious because of its numerous brothels, the Bowies moved away, and Pike Street's name was changed to the more poetic Waverly Place, in a vain attempt to return the area to greater respectability."

Although Waverly/Pike was in the heart of Chinatown, after Ah Toy departed the whorehouses located on it appear to have featured only white prostitutes. In his 1876 book, *Lights and Shades in San Francisco*, B. E. Lloyd writes, "Waverly Place, or 'Pike' street, is notorious for the boldness of its vice . . . At any hour of the day or night, sickly, vice-worn women, abundantly painted and powdered and gaudily attired in the vain attempt to restore their lost charms, may be seen upon the thresholds or lounging by the open windows." Since Lloyd did not describe these women as Chinese, it is safe to assume they were white.

The infamous 1885 "vice map" of Chinatown prepared by the San Francisco Board of Supervisors, which depicts every brothel, gambling den, and opium parlor in Chinatown, is more definitive. It shows no fewer than twelve houses of "white prostitution" (and no Chinese ones) on the first block of Waverly between Sacramento and Clay. The map shows about eighty houses of "Chinese prostitution" elsewhere in Chinatown, mostly clustered just above and below Dupont (Grant) between Jackson and Pacific.

Pike Street already had an unsavory reputation. But it was after its name was changed to Waverly Place that the little street really became synonymous with murder and mayhem. The rise of the fighting tongs, secretive Chinese mafias whose hatchet-carrying foot soldiers, so-called highbinders, were sworn to carry out whatever murderous mayhem their leaders ordered, was responsible for the bloodiest chapter in the street's history.

## THE HATCHET MEN OF WAVERLY PLACE

During the brutal heyday of the fighting tongs, Waverly Place was infamous. "People all over California and the West, and eventually in all corners of the United States, came to know the names of the squalid Chinatown alleys which were the scenes of murders or pitched tong battles," as Richard Dillon writes in *Hatchet Men*, one of the most fascinating books ever written about San Francisco. Of those labyrinthine alleys, the most notorious was Waverly. "Escape was easy in the alleyways, particularly by night," Dillon writes. "Waverly's stygian blackness was hardly cut at all by the feeble street lamp, a few strings of paper lanterns, the dim light leaking through dusty, curtained windows, and the glowing braziers of the curbside foodsellers."

In 1875, a pitched battle on Waverly took place between the two principal warring tongs, the Suey Sing and Kwong Duck. Like many tong wars, this one erupted over a woman, in this case a prostitute known as the "Golden Peach." When the hatchets, knives, and guns had finished their bloody work, five highbinders lay dead, with twelve wounded.

The most famous of all Chinatown killings, the 1897 murder of crime boss Little Pete, took place on Ross Alley, just steps away from Waverly. The two

murderers escaped by running into a building at 123 Waverly Place—next door to the current location of the Tian Hou Temple.

Appropriately, when the tong wars eventually came to an end, peace was formalized on Waverly Place. In 1913, the Wo Ping Woey Peace Association was formed, and the warring tongs gathered at its Waverly building to sign a truce.

Over the following decades, Waverly Place was still from time to time associated with crime—but of a far more innocuous variety. In his memoir *China 2227*, Lyle Jan recalls how in 1936 his family moved into a third-floor apartment at 745 Grant Avenue. Their apartment's kitchen had a door that connected with the common hallway of another building at 46 Waverly Place. Occasionally, friends of Jan's father, runners working for an illegal Oakland Chinatown gambling syndicate, would suspect they were being tailed by cops from the Chinatown Squad. "The runner would come up to our floor and if someone was home, ask permission to leave by the Waverly Place exit," Jan writes. "His excuse would be that he wanted a shortcut to where he was heading for. We all knew the real reason but pretended we didn't. He just wanted to lose the cop who was tailing him."

## CHINATOWN'S MAKEOVER

The Tian Hou Temple and its adjoining buildings on Waverly Place make up one of the best-known streetscapes in Chinatown. To the casual observer, they look like a row of authentic Chinese buildings, complete with exotic curved roofs, bright colors, wrought-iron balconies, and intricate columns. Yet these buildings, like most of the others in Chinatown, are not authentically Chinese at all but a weird amalgam of Chinese design elements and Western construction techniques. They are, in effect, false fronts: Chinatown is one big Potemkin village. The story of how this neighborhood came to look the way it does is a unique example of a community rebranding and remaking itself to survive and prosper.

Before 1906, the buildings in Chinatown were drab and colorless. It looked pretty much like the rest of San Francisco, except that its alleys were dirtier and more convoluted. It also had a serious image problem, partly due to racism but also partly self-inflicted. Most residents of Chinatown were law-abiding citizens, but the quarter's byzantine byways were filled with brothels staffed by enslaved prostitutes, opium dens, and gambling parlors. As we've seen, the violent tongs that ran these vice rackets engaged in incessant bloody turf wars. Although Chinatown was a popular tourist attraction—in no small part because of its reputation for exotic sinfulness—few would visit it after dark without a police escort. Those fears were exaggerated but not entirely unfounded.

City officials had been trying to get rid of Chinatown almost as soon as it sprang up in the area around Sacramento Street during the Gold Rush. This impulse was driven primarily by racism and xenophobia, but it was exacerbated by Chinese separatism. The overwhelming majority of early Chinese immigrants had no interest in becoming Americans, let alone assimilating. They had come to "Gold Mountain," as California was known, strictly to make their fortune. They regarded Americans as barbarians and intended to return home as soon as possible. Indeed, when they died, many of them had their bones shipped home so they could be buried in their native soil. Their refusal to integrate did not endear them to Americans. Moreover, working-class whites increasingly resented Chinese laborers, who would work for a fraction of the money whites made. Finally, Chinatown's deserved reputation as a hotbed of vice caused the chorus calling for the removal of the neighborhood to swell—notwithstanding the fact that whites both connived at that vice and profited from it.

The 1906 earthquake, which destroyed Chinatown along with almost all of downtown San Francisco, presented city fathers with what appeared to be a golden opportunity to get rid of the quarter once and for all. A high-level Subcommittee on the Permanent Relocation of Chinatown suggested that Chinatown be moved to remote Hunters Point, a longtime dumping ground for undesirable industries that after World War II became an isolated, impoverished black ghetto. But the Chinese community successfully resisted, quickly rebuilding and flexing hitherto unused political clout. The city's attempt to remove Chinatown failed.

At the same time, however, Chinese leaders realized that they needed to clean up Chinatown—both superficially and substantially. For decades, vice had been the main economic driver in the quarter. But the power of the mafia-like tongs that controlled the vice rackets was fading, and community notables realized that Chinatown's future lay not in gambling, prostitution, and opium but in Chinese restaurants (of which there were relatively few before the earthquake) and tourism. Chinatown was ready for its makeover.

To transform ominous, sinful old Chinatown into an exotic, family-friendly place, Chinese leaders hired white architects to turn the neighborhood into a phantasmagoric "Oriental City." They employed traditional Chinese motifs such as pagoda towers, massive curved roofs, multitiered eaves, wrought-iron balconies, brilliant red, green, and yellow colors, a profusion of columns, and curled-up corners, but they were purely decorative: unlike their counterparts in authentic Chinese architecture, they had no structural function.

The illusion proved wildly successful. The new, Disneyland-like Chinatown was far more popular and profitable than the old one. And deeper changes also took place. White prejudice against Chinese lessened, and increasing numbers of Chinese began to consider themselves Americans. Vice faded out: the last tong war took place in 1921, the last slave girl raid in 1925.

Vice and violence were not completely eradicated from Chinatown. In a modern version of the old tong wars, a bloody rivalry between one gang called the Joe Boys and another called the Wah Ching erupted in the 1960s and 1970s, culminating in a 1977 gang shooting at the Golden Dragon restaurant on Washington and Grant that left five innocent people dead. But thanks to more effective policing and sociological changes in the neighborhood and among new immigrants, the "Golden Dragon Massacre" proved to be one of the last outbreaks of gang violence in the quarter. Today, Chinatown has virtually no crime.

# CHAPTER 5

# CALHOUN TERRACE

## THE HAUNTED BALCONY OF TELEGRAPH HILL

CALHOUN TERRACE IS haunted, and not by garden-variety ghosts. The spirits that hover around this short, spectacular split-level street near the summit of Telegraph Hill are numerous and deeply odd, including the flickering shades of two of the finest movies ever shot here, a theater impresario who made money in a singularly cracked way, a creepy film noir, a legacy of world-class partying, and the two most unethical businessmen ever to give a bad name to the San Francisco Chamber of Commerce. In fact, the evil deeds of the last-mentioned characters turned a section of Calhoun into a literal ghost.

Calhoun is a stunning balcony of a street that looks out to downtown and the East Bay over the precipitous eastern face of Telegraph Hill. That section of the cliff is almost vertical, and it also drops off at the southern end of Calhoun, creating a dead end.

But the rock face wasn't always like that. The Gray brothers made it that way.

George and Harry Gray were the city's leading quarrymen in the late nineteenth and early twentieth centuries. Rich and politically connected, they took advantage of corruption and nonexistent law enforcement to merrily blast away in residential areas even after they were repeatedly ordered to stop, blithely destroying houses and seriously injuring people..

Their first quarry was at Green and Sansome streets, below what was then called Calhoun Street. Before the Gray brothers began blasting, Calhoun used to connect Green and Union streets. But their explosions not only blasted a shoemaker's house at the corner of Union and Calhoun off its foundations but obliterated the entire east side of Calhoun and Green and much of the west, creating a 125-foot-high precipice where the street once ran. The brothers defied a court order and continued blasting on the Fourth of July, blaming the explosions, with truly world-class chutzpah, on cannon fire from the Presidio. Eventually, in a gratifying example of karmic fallout, the brothers' quarrying business failed and an unpaid employee shot one of the brothers to death. The employee was acquitted and walked out of the courtroom to the cheers of a hundred supporters.

## THE SCRAMBLED SAGA OF DOC ROBINSON

The oldest house on Calhoun Terrace, and one of the oldest in San Francisco, is number nine, built in 1854 by David G. "Doc" Robinson. Robinson was one of the most fascinating characters to emerge from the city's Gold Rush years—and considering the competition, this makes him a most intriguing egg indeed. A Maine native and graduate of Yale University, Robinson was bitten by the theater bug on the East Coast before immigrating to California in 1849. Casting about for ways to make money, he hit upon one of the most unlikely entrepreneurial

schemes in the history of a city that specialized in them. Realizing that eggs were scarce and expensive, Robinson and a partner sailed out to the shark-haunted Farallon Islands, twenty-eight miles outside the Golden Gate, and gathered eggs from the vast flocks of murres that nested on its steep crags. Notwithstanding the unappetizing fact that the yolks of murre eggs are red, Robinson sold them for a huge profit to city restaurants, using the proceeds to open a pharmacy on Portsmouth Square—hence his nickname "Doc."

Other entrepreneurs followed Robinson to the Farallons, leading to turf disputes and ultimately to the hardest-boiled conflict in the city's history, the Egg War of 1863, in which an egger was shot to death off the desolate islands.

But Robinson's true passion was theater. He became famous for his satiric skits and songs, in which he would gently (and not-so-gently) lampoon the instant city's leading figures, as well as subjects ranging from opera to politics to the Gold Rush itself. Robinson opened a theater called the Dramatic Museum, an informal little space in which audience members would interject comments and sing along with the musical numbers. Robinson's skills as actor, writer, impresario, and chronicler of the town's eccentricities made him so beloved he was elected an alderman and for a time was considered the leading candidate for the mayor's office.

Robinson's next-door neighbor at 5 Calhoun (the building no longer exists) was a minor actor named June Booth, the son of the most famous tragedian of the day, Junius Booth, and the older brother of a more talented actor, Edwin. (A third brother, John Wilkes, would upstage them all with his murderous performance at Ford's Theatre in Washington, D.C.).

The Booths and other thespians, possibly including one of the most beloved actors ever to appear in San Francisco, Lotta Crabtree, had uproarious times at Robinson's house. One of their favorite high jinks was watering their jointly owned horse with champagne poured out of a silver salver. From his widow's walk, Robinson could look down upon his new theater, the twenty-two-hundred-seat American. Because it was built at the water's edge, the entire building sank two inches under the weight of its audience on opening night.

Robinson's moment in San Francisco's theatrical sun was brief. Another, equally colorful entrepreneur, a former New York City hack driver named Tom Maguire, opened a rival theater called the Jenny Lind and eclipsed Robinson. Undaunted, the irrepressible Doc headed east to seek greater successes on the histrionic boards. He had reached Alabama when he contracted a fever and died.

## CALHOUN AND THE SILVER SCREEN

Hugging the edge of an almost vertical cliff overlooking the bay and downtown, with Coit Tower looming above it, Calhoun Terrace has one of the most spectacular settings of any street in San Francisco. So it's not surprising that numerous movies have used it and the intersection above it as a location. The list includes the greatest film ever set in the city, *Vertigo*, another great, *Days of Wine and Roses*, and a creepy 1952 noir called *The Sniper*.

In the first two films, the north end of Calhoun and the bay behind it appear in the background, in almost identical east-facing shots taken from higher ground at Union and Montgomery. (Weirdly, even the action in the two scenes is virtually identical: in each, the male protagonist drives up in a car with a female character who lives in the same building.)

In *The Sniper*, Calhoun plays a more central role. The film's protagonist is a troubled World War II vet who works for a dry-cleaning company. A subtle hint that he may be suffering from unresolved anger issues involving women occurs in the movie's opening scene, when he aims the telescopic scope of his army rifle at a young woman who is kissing her boyfriend on an exterior stairway across the street from his Filbert Street apartment. He refrains from pulling the trigger, but his homicidal impulses have only been deferred. When he delivers a dress to another woman who lives at 36 Calhoun, on the street's lower level, they are triggered.

During their brief interaction, this woman makes two unfortunate mistakes. First, she flirts with him. Then, when her boyfriend calls, she hustles him unceremoniously out the back door. Our hero does not take this well. His depression having now escalated to full-blown misogynistic dementia, he returns and shoots her dead. As his fate draws near, he runs down the alley that I live on, leaving a trail of murderous misogyny that is fortunately only visible to fans of obscure film noirs.

## DANCING ON THE BRINK OF THE WORLD

A tantalizing fragment of poetry from the city's original inhabitants, the Ohlone Indians, has come down to us: "Dancing on the brink of the world." The motto could apply to Calhoun Terrace. From the beginning, the tiny street perched on a near-vertical cliff face has been one of the city's great party streets.

Calhoun's let-it-rip tradition started in 1854, when a colony of pleasure-loving actors would gather at Doc Robinson's house for assorted alcohol-fueled fun and games. (Appropriately, when the 1906 fire threatened the building, its owner saved it by smothering sparks with wine-soaked rags—or so the story goes.) Later, the street hosted perhaps the most legendary party locale in San Francisco, a multiunit building at the corner of Calhoun and Union known simply as the Compound. In the early twentieth century, a band of bohemian writers and artists lived in the dozen studios of what disapproving types called "the rabbit warren." A new owner named Ian Hoeffler bought the property in 1937 and brought in tenants who belonged to increasingly higher tax brackets, but they continued to party. When Calhoun was divided into two levels in 1939-40 by the Works Progress Administration (one of many WPA projects that improved and beautified the city during the Depression), they held big block parties on different levels—a tradition that continues to this day. A flyer for a 1954 party on Lower Calhoun Terrace announced, "PLEASE HEED: Local ordinances being what they are . . . all liquor will have to be contained within, not upon, the person; and the wearing of apparel of the opposite sex will be more than somewhat frowned upon!"

The good times came to an end when Hoeffler sold the building to a developer

who razed it and erected the uninspired building that stands there now. According to David Myrick's *San Francisco's Telegraph Hill*, Hoeffler painted the old building a shocking pink just before he gave his tenants their eviction notices. The inhabitants held an epic two-day party before they were sadly forced to depart forever. One pretty blond woman said, "I've had the best time of my life here." Another removed the doors to her apartment and took them with her, saying, "They'll be my portals to the past."

## WHEN TELEGRAPH HILL WAS POOR

Today, shacks on Telegraph Hill are worth millions of dollars. But for more than eighty years after the Gold Rush, the hill was a working-class neighborhood, inhabited by longshoremen, firemen, laborers, and storekeepers, many of them Italian, Irish, and Hispanic, along with a smattering of bohemians.

The main reason was accessibility. Until the 1920s and 1930s, most of the hill was not accessible by automobile. But the neighborhood's reputation as a multi-ethnic enclave also probably served as a deterrent: In 1897, the author Frank Norris wrote, "Here on this wartlike protuberance above the city's roof, a great milling is going on, and a fusing of peoples, and in a few more generations the Celt and the

Italian, the Mexican and the Chinaman, the Negro and the Portuguese . . . will be fused into one type. And what a type it will be." This was not a demographic mixture likely to bring in those listed in the *Blue Book*. Finally, much of the housing stock in the neighborhood was old and primitive, flimsy wooden cottages with bad plumbing and single-burner stoves.

These factors kept Telegraph Hill from attracting the wealthy. In houses on Calhoun and Alta and Montgomery now occupied by C-suite tech executives, financiers, and high-end lawyers, dockworkers used to watch the bay for the approach of ships that meant work, descending the steep wooden steps to head to the piers. One worker who lived on Alta could recognize the type of cargo a ship was carrying by the blasts on its horn.

Because it was inconvenient to haul groceries up to the summit, a half-dozen food markets did business on a two-block stretch of Montgomery Street above Calhoun. An early twentieth-century photograph shows two little girls walking on the unpaved street on the way to two different stores. One of the girls appears to be about four years old. At Meisel's grocery, which opened in 1881 at the corner of Union and Montgomery, housewives used to line up at five in the morning to buy ten cents' worth of whiskey so that their husbands could fill the flasks they took to work in their lunch pails.

The end of this impecunious era was announced in 1923, when Telegraph Hill Boulevard was constructed, making it possible for cars to ascend to the summit. Modern apartment houses soon followed. In 1936, a piece in the *New York Times* lamented the end of the old Telegraph Hill, under a headline that has run, with minor variations, every few years since: "San Francisco's Historic Bohemian Quarter Succumbs to the Forces of Economics and Modernism."

The eternally-recurring headline is always right. The bohemians have been leaving the hill forever. But thanks to rent control, a house purchased in the Jurassic era, or just a cockroach-like refusal to leave the seacoast of Bohemia even if it means living in a cockroach-sized apartment, there are still a few of us hiding in the crevices.

## THE HILL FOUND AROUND THE WORLD

The quarrying of Telegraph Hill carved out its sheer eastern face, but it also had another, much odder consequence.

Much of the rock blasted from Telegraph Hill was used for ballast by ships that had emptied their holds in San Francisco and could not find return cargoes. After they returned to their home ports, their captains recycled the ballast as paving material and fill. Which means that streets in Valparaiso and Sydney, New York and Liverpool, are paved with Telegraph Hill graywacke. Not just its fame but the hill itself is spread all over the world.

CHAPTER 6

# LOMBARD STREET

## HUMPHREYS' CASTLE

THE NORTH SLOPE of Russian Hill, famous for the curving block of Lombard Street known as "the Crookedest Street in the World," is one of San Francisco's swankiest neighborhoods. That was also true in the 1850s and 1860s, when the hill's northern spine on Hyde Street around Lombard and Chestnut streets featured a number of elegant homes. A few of those splendid buildings remain, but most were either destroyed in the 1906 earthquake and fire or torn down in the twentieth century.

One of Russian Hill's lost houses was a beautiful 1852 southern plantation–style mansion on the northeast corner of Chestnut and Hyde, built by a prominent early San Franciscan named William Squire Clark. In 1847, Clark built the city's first wharf off a rocky promontory at what is now Broadway and Battery. The promontory became known as Clark's Point. Flush with money he made from the wharf (which enjoyed a monopoly until 1849), in 1848 Clark purchased the entire summit block bounded by Broadway, Vallejo, Taylor, and Jones, six 50-vara lots, for $37.50 each. (A vara, slightly less than a yard, was the standard lot measurement used in the Spanish and Mexican eras, and continued to be used for a while in the American era.) It was a shrewd real estate deal: he held the land through the Gold Rush and sold it in 1853 for $5,000.

Four years after his extremely profitable purchase, Clark built his magnificent house on Chestnut and Hyde out of old ships' timbers. In 1868, he sold it to a

surveyor named William Penn Humphreys. Because of its castellated cornices, Gothic ornamentation, and octagonal tower, it became known as Humphreys' Castle. The house remained in the Humphreys family until the late 1920s, when it was sold. Plans to tear it down and erect an apartment building on the site aroused fierce opposition. The de Young Museum expressed interest in preserving it as an example of one of the oldest houses in San Francisco, and the house's new owner even offered to give it away to anyone who would move it. Sadly, this early architectural preservation battle failed, and Humphreys' Castle was torn down in 1948. A modern building now stands there.

This ritzy post–Gold Rush interlude was something of an anomaly. Hard as it may be to believe now, for many years Russian Hill, like its fellow downtown hills Telegraph and Nob, was not a universally desired address. (The one exception, as described on page 167, was Rincon Hill.) With their steep eastern faces, they were simply too hard to get to. However, Russian Hill always had its share of well-to-do residents and mansions. The views from its summits proved irresistible even in the days residents had to go two or three blocks out of their way to get home.

# CARL HENRY'S LONG AND WINDING ROAD

In 1860, Russian Hill received its first tourist attraction, when a Captain David Dobson opened an observatory at Lombard and Hyde, charging twenty-five cents for the view. By the 1870s, the area around Humphreys' Castle had become less patrician and more middle-class, although some upper-crust types such as George and Phoebe Hearst, parents of William Randolph Hearst, lived there. Not as many bohemians were drawn to this more expensive part of Russian Hill as to the summit on Vallejo Street (see page 115), but a few writers and artists did take up residence here. A flamboyant Hearst columnist who wrote under the nom de plume Annie Laurie (her real name was Winifred Bonfils) lived in an earthquake shack on Lombard Street. (After the 1906 earthquake and fire, the city built more than 5,000 small wooden cottages to house displaced working-class people. These "earthquake shacks" were initially located in official refugee camps, but their occupants were later allowed to move them.) Bonfils was a prominent member of a tribe of female scribes known as "sob sisters" for their tear-jerking exposés: as detailed on page 115, one of her stories led to the creation of the city's Emergency Hospital System. Bonfils was so beloved that when she died, her body was laid out in state in City Hall. Fanny Stevenson, Robert Louis Stevenson's widow, lived in the house on the northwest corner of Lombard and Hyde. She was often seen wearing flowing Polynesian robes and wandering in her garden.

But the early resident who left the most indelible mark on Lombard Street was a man named Carl Henry. Henry started out as a newsboy in the Financial District before cofounding the Owl Drug Company and making a pile in insurance. In 1904, he bought his first lot on Russian Hill, in the 1000 block of Chestnut Street below Hyde. After the earthquake he began buying up more lots on Lombard and Chestnut streets, expanding an earthquake shack that was on one property. By the 1920s, he owned half the block between Hyde and Leavenworth.

Henry sank $70,000 into the magnificent gardens on his lot on the corner of Lombard and Hyde, planting rare plants and trees and installing a lily pond, a rose garden, and a wine cellar. A widower, Henry enjoyed living large: he had an Airedale dog, a $100,000 yacht, a large staff of Japanese servants, and a Burns security guard who patrolled the grounds.

Henry intended to turn his gardens into a public park and lease it to the city. But his luck ran out after the Wall Street crash of 1929, the same year he remarried at age fifty-three. When he died four years later, his yacht was valued at just

$8,000, his clothes at $1.50, and he owed $16 for a prescription to Owl Drug, the company he cofounded. Henry's dream of a grand city park atop Russian Hill died when his estate was sold. But he did leave an enduring legacy: he was partly responsible for the creation of the crooked street (see page 63).

## WHEN GOATS CLIMBED LOMBARD STREET

A wonderful evocation of life on Lombard Street, before and after the curves were put in, is provided by a woman named Hettie Belle Marcus, who lived on the street for decades. In 1920, she and her husband had been living in Menlo Park but wanted to move to San Francisco. They saw a FOR RENT sign on 1040 Lombard and rented it from the owner, Mrs. Albert Pissis, wife of the famous architect who designed the Hibernia Bank and the Mechanics' Institute.

"And so we moved to Lombard Street," Marcus writes in a brief memoir. "At that time, the original great cobbles paved the street—which was an unusable 27 percent grade. On either side of the street were straight, rough cement sidewalks with wooden cleats nailed across them at intervals. These were never in good repair. Between the cobblestones, enough earth had collected to encourage a variety of wildflowers, dandelions, etc. These greens frequently encouraged a herd of goats—supposedly tethered in a great field off Chestnut Street where the Art Institute now stands. They would come solemnly up the hill, dragging their chains and stakes, enjoying their find."

(Russian Hill was not the only now swanky San Francisco hill that was home to herds of goats in the early twentieth century and earlier. In the 1920s, a woman named Milanelli Cosenza kept a herd of goats in the backyard of her house at 1220 Kearny Street on Telegraph Hill, which she would lead through a back lot, down Castle Street, and up to a foraging patch on Montgomery Street, calling out their Italian names as she walked and returning for them at dusk. Cosenza sold the fresh goat milk on the hill, milking her charges right at the customer's door. In 1928, after a neighbor complained that the goats were eating her flowers, the city banished goats from Telegraph Hill.)

The Marcuses bought the house the next year. One of their neighbors, an Italian widower named Mr. Maisch who was head of "trouble" for the San Francisco Water Department, lived in "a funny little house below street level," where, like almost all of the Italian families in nearby North Beach, he would make his own wine. Marcus recalls being invited on Sunday morning to sample it from a huge barrel in his garden. Maisch would already be feeling no pain. A communal wine press would be hauled from house to house and they would hear the Italians singing as they pressed the wine. They would dump the leftover skins, seeds, and stems in a vacant lot at the bottom of the block, on the southwest corner of Lombard and Leavenworth.

Considering the glee with which hordes of tourists now congregate on that spot, happily taking pictures of one of the most famous streets in the country, it seems appropriate that singing Italians once rolled wine casks down a chicken-steps sidewalk and emptied them on the corner.

## HOW LOMBARD STREET GOT ITS CURVES

For decades, cobblestoned, 27 percent–grade Lombard Street was inaccessible to cars. (Today there are much steeper streets than this in San Francisco, but cars have improved.) Although this kept the street secluded, it also reduced property values.

Carl Henry, who owned half the block, proposed solving the problem by installing curves, thus lessening the grade. A civil engineer named Parsons hired by the Merchants Association had proposed such an idea in 1905, but it was never implemented.

In 1922, a city engineer named Clyde Healey figured out how to implement Henry's—or Parsons's—idea. Legendary city engineer Michael O'Shaughnessy, who built the dam at Hetch Hetchy that provides San Francisco's water, summoned Lombard Street property owners to City Hall and told them that Healey had had a "brainstorm" and was sure he could make the street accessible to cars. O'Shaughnessy said the city would pay for the installation of the curves if they would pay for the sidewalks, landscaping, and upkeep.

The plan went through, but not without a classic bit of San Francisco neighborhood infighting. Two sisters named Wolf refused to pay if veronica was planted (!), and other homeowners also refused to contribute for one reason or another. According to Hettie Bell Marcus, for many years only she and one other property owner paid their upkeep dues.

The curves were installed on Lombard Street in 1922. It had eight curves and the grade had been reduced to 18.18 percent. Nineteen thousand bricks were used on the eight-hundred-foot-long street. It was a two-way street and remained so until 1939, when it became one-way.

For almost forty years, Lombard Street was no more of a tourist destination than San Francisco's other curvy street, Vermont on Potrero Hill, whose curves were installed in 1928. Lombard's prominence was triggered when a resident named Peter Bercut (a park commissioner and avid horseman, he is known to explorers of Golden Gate Park because the Bercut Equitation Field was named after him) planted hydrangeas. A 1961 postcard of the street with the brilliantly colored flowers—all 1,099 of them—opened the floodgates.

Today, more than two million cars a year go down Lombard, with as many as 350 descending it in an hour. Hundreds of tourists gather at the bottom and top, and traffic on Lombard Street in the summer is often backed up all the way to Van Ness. All of these tourists attract criminals: an epidemic of auto break-ins around the block was highlighted in 2018, when the *San Francisco Chronicle* ran a front-page photo of a man brazenly reaching into a broken car window.

Fed-up residents have periodically asked the city to close it to auto traffic. The idea was considered twice in the 1970s, but rejected. In 2019, a fee and reservation system for the street was proposed, in which drivers would be assessed $5 ($10 on weekends) to drive down it. The bill was approved by the Board of Supervisors and the state assembly, but vetoed by Governor Gavin Newsom, who said it would be unfair to poorer citizens. Driving down the "Crookedest Street in the World" seems destined to remain as essential to the San Francisco bucket list as a visit to the Golden Gate Bridge, a walk through Chinatown, or a ride on the cable cars. Which means that living on once-bucolic Lombard Street is never going to be even remotely peaceful.

# CHAPTER 7

# THE ROCK HOUSE

## ROCK CITY

ONE OF THE singular joys of San Francisco is its rocks. Like an ancient, permanent June, they keep busting out all over. No other city I know of has such a wonderfully aggressive geology. Graywacke and serpentine and radiolarian chert and pillow basalt pop up everywhere in this town—from massive peaks to tiny outcroppings, from sides of hills to jagged canyons, from seaside cliffs to individual boulders. And these igneous, metamorphic, and sedimentary guests show up in the most unexpected places—not just in parks or on the coastline or on higher ground but in industrial zones, leafy upper-crust streets, banal neighborhoods of 1930s tract homes, and everything in between. I have been walking San Francisco for fifty years, and it feels as though every time I wander around, I discover some rock outcropping I've never seen.

Once you really focus in on San Francisco's ubiquitous rocks, they completely alter the way you see the city. Its apparent permanence and solidity is revealed to be a false front, a thin veneer stretched over something much bigger and more unknowable. There's something delicious about this, like an unexpected key change in a familiar tune. You may be strolling like a flaneur through downtown, deep in the human hive. But once you know about the rocks, one part of you is hiking in the mountains.

The weirder the juxtaposition of rock and urban setting, the tastier the dissonance. In terms of the sheer value of the real estate being hogged, the weirdest may

be a large graywacke outcropping on Powell between Sacramento and Clay, less than two blocks from one of the most famous intersections in the city, California and Powell, and just up from Joice Street. From this corner, one block below the Fairmont and the Mark Hopkins hotels on the summit of Nob Hill, there's a fabled view down Powell to Union Square and an even more fabled view down California to the Financial District and the bay. Cable cars clank up both streets and cross at the intersection. It's the only place in the city where the cable crossing is manually controlled, by a man in a little green kiosk on the southeast corner. That kiosk is a good candidate for San Francisco ground zero. And it's surrounded by hotels, private clubs, and condominiums that bear commensurate price tags.

Which makes it somewhat disconcerting to walk about a hundred yards north and come upon a vacant lot with a huge rocky outcropping in it, enclosed by a chain-link fence. This untouched piece of Nob Hill has been standing there since at least 1971 and probably since 19,710 B.C., apparently no more capable of being monetized now than it was when short-faced bears and American lions prowled Nob Hill.

Of the many other surreal rock apparitions around town, the one with the best combination of mind-boggling history and obscure location is a large boulder in the backyard of a house on Delta Street in Visitacion Valley. This rock marks the place where, on July 2, 1777, a party of Spanish soldiers and priests traveling north to the Presidio in San Francisco got lost in heavy fog and camped overnight. When they awoke, they found they were in a beautiful valley, which they named Visitacion. After this, according to local lore, they celebrated Mass, using the boulder for an altar.

## HOUSES THAT ROCK

Since rocks are constantly barging in where they're least wanted in San Francisco, it's not surprising that they are frequently found next to, under, or even inside buildings. There used to be a garage on a street in Bernal Heights that contained not a car (unless the driver was Wilma Flintstone) but a garage-sized rock. A little-known and incredibly elegant modernist building in the woods near the Fairy Gates above the University of California–San Francisco sits next to a smooth boulder that would not be out of place in Yosemite. And there's a building on Church Street near Dolores Park resting on a rock formation that looks larger than the house.

But the most dramatic case of rock-meets-house in San Francisco is the massive serpentine extrusion under the "Rock House," a consummately strange building at Mariposa and Utah. If this greenish outcropping looks oddly similar to the rocks

you see as you drive down Innes Avenue in Hunters Point, or the rocky platform of the new mint at Market and Duboce, or the formations under the anchorage of the Golden Gate Bridge, it's because they're all made of the same rock, serpentine—which happens to be the California state rock.

All of those sites lie within something geologists call the Fort Point–Hunters Point mélange zone. There are two mélange zones in San Francisco, both of which run diagonally from southeast to northwest across the city (the other is the City College mélange zone). These zones were created when the two tectonic plates that meet near San Francisco scraped across each other during the titanic process known as subduction, grinding up some of the rock found in the plates. As the name implies, a mélange zone is a mixture of hard, or "resistant," and soft rocks; geologist Doris Sloan describes it as "like a geologic chocolate pudding with raisins, nuts, and marshmallows (the resistant blocks) mixed into it." Serpentine, a hard, metamorphic rock (one altered from its original state by high heat and pressure during subduction), is the resistant nut in the Fort Point–Hunters Point pudding.

The serpentine outcropping at Mariposa and Utah runs at least one hundred feet long north to south and eighty feet west to east and is about fifteen feet high. It's not the biggest outcropping of serpentine in San Francisco by a long shot, but it's the biggest one under a house. If the aforementioned Wilma Flintstone had a spare $7 million, this would be her mansion of choice. It is the granddaddy of the city's residential rock platforms.

## THE ROCK HOUSE

The Rock House is one of the most unusual buildings in the city, but very few people, even those who live in Potrero Hill or the Mission, know about it. That's because of the Bayshore Freeway, which cuts off both of the two streets on whose corner it stands, turning the area around it into an isolated enclave that only residents or urban wanderers would have any reason to go into. Ironically, once you know about the Rock House, you see it looming up to the west every time you drive down the freeway. And only then do you realize just what an odd piece of land it stands on—a peculiar, orphaned little piece of Potrero Hill that's separated from the main part of the hill by the freeway. This anomalous quasi-island—call it Potrero Hill West—even has its own pedestrian walkway connecting it to the "mainland." Just north of that walkway, on Utah Street, is a mini park with, of all things, a bocce court.

The Rock House has a history as peculiar as its surroundings. The imposing three-story, 6,645-square-foot building on its 12,500-square-foot lot (more than a quarter of an acre) was built in 1911 to house an early social work institution called the Society for Helping Boys. The Society for Helping Boys is forgotten today, but it was founded by an illustrious figure in San Francisco's cultural history named Joseph Worcester. Worcester was a Swedenborgian minister and an amateur architect, who many people thought bore a remarkable resemblance to Jesus Christ. In 1889, Worcester built a cottage on Vallejo Street on the summit of Russian Hill that may be the first example of a consciously "rustic" house in San Francisco. That cottage is gone, but two adjoining shingle-style houses Worcester planned are still standing. To eyes accustomed to simple, wood-shingled houses, there is nothing obviously note-worthy about them, but they represent the beginning of the end of the Victorian era in San Francisco architecture. Willis Polk, who also despised Victorian architecture, lived in the spectacular wood-shingled house across the street.

Worcester started the Society for Helping Boys in 1904 to house and provide education for "friendless working boys," ages sixteen and up, from broken homes or troubled backgrounds. Worcester apparently had his friend Bruce Porter prepare plans for the building. Porter, who also served on the society's board, was a polymath designer, artist, and writer famous for launching the irreverent fin de siècle literary magazine the *Lark* with writer and provocateur Gelett Burgess, who lived just a few steps away from Worcester on Vallejo Street (see page 158).

By 1950, the boys' home had been acquired by San Francisco State College, which at the time was a ramshackle cluster of buildings around Buchanan and Waller (for years, the only viable classroom was located in a former orphanage's chapel). "The Rock," as it continued to be called, was the college's only campus-run housing for nonveterans. It housed twenty-five to thirty men who did all their own cooking and cleaning, under the supervision of a student employee and his wife.

The Rock's odd higher education interregnum lasted only until 1954, when the big house was occupied for a year by one Robert Marmorstein, described in the city directory as a salesman. Marmorstein was succeeded in 1955–1956 by a couple named Douglas and Colleen Carter. Their sojourn also lasted only a year. The building was vacant from 1957 until 1960.

The vacant building on its massive rock platform had already had a very strange history. So it made perfect sense that its next chapter would be inaugurated by a psychic.

## FROM A HAUNTED HOUSE TO A $7.7 MILLION MANSION

An odd, delightful—and almost eternal—figure on the San Francisco art and design scene was a man named Rudolph Schaeffer. Schaeffer was the first person to teach prismatic color theory and the first non-Japanese to write a book about flower arranging. Born in 1886, he opened his first design school in Chinatown (!) in 1926 (!), giving it the heavily Germanic name the Rudolph Schaeffer School of Rhythmo-Chromatic Design. In 1951, Schaeffer—who had wisely changed his institution's name to the Rudolph Schaeffer School of Design—moved it to Union Street in North Beach. The school had money problems—a recurring theme in Schaeffer's professional life—and when the building was sold in 1958, Schaeffer's friends advised the seventy-two-year-old to close it.

But Schaeffer insisted that the school must continue. A 1979 article on Schaeffer in *California Living* magazine relates what happened next. "Everyone looked for a proper building. None was found. But Schaeffer, a man of many media, knew a medium, 'a real psychic in Carmel.' The psychic lady was consulted. 'No problem,' she said, and described a deserted building on Potrero Hill, 'with many windows on the west side, overlooking a cliff and a backyard gone to native grass.'

"Schaeffer found the building, called The Rock, a former boys' home, at 2255 Mariposa Street. Money came forward: The Rock has housed the Schaeffer school for the last 18 years."

Schaeffer lived in a cottage he had built at the rear of the property, where he designed and tended a "Peace Garden."

It is just one of many odd facts about the Rock House that two of San Francisco's better-known designers, Bruce Porter and Rudolph Schaeffer, were both involved with it in totally unconnected ways.

Schaeffer was eventually ousted by the board from the school he had run for more than sixty years, but he lived to garner civic recognition for his long and illustrious career. On June 26, 1986, Schaeffer's 100th birthday, the city of San Francisco declared Rudolph Schaeffer Day and celebrated it with great fanfare. Schaeffer died in 1988, just before his 102nd birthday.

When Schaeffer's school went out of business in 1984, the Rock's long run of institutional oddness came to an end. In 1987, a New York art dealer and collector named Allen Stone bought the Rock House compound and completely remodeled it. In 2014, the building with the weird and wonderful past now entered the still weirder, but not so wonderful unless you are a low-numbered Google employee, world of contemporary San Francisco real estate. It was sold in 2014 for $3.9 million and is now used as a three-unit residence. Whoever bought it did all right financially: its estimated value in late 2019 was $7.7 million.

For a building anchored to bedrock, the Rock House has had a wild ride. When it was built, the city was just recovering from the earthquake, Potrero Hill was semirural, the freeway was fifty years in the future, and the downtown skyline barely existed. Today, whoever is looking out the window from its thirty-foot-high great room beholds the SalesForce Tower, like a colossal rocket ship that has just touched down from planet Billionaire, blasting flames on a shell-shocked city. But it's all part of the passing show. The Rock House has seen ministers and orphans and students and plutocrats, and sooner or later the movie will start running backward, and in the end the whole building will probably be covered with water. When it does, the big slab of metamorphic rock under the house, forged far below the earth's surface millions of years ago, will still be there.

# CHAPTER 8

# HUNTINGTON PARK

## THE JEWEL OF NOB HILL

BECAUSE OF THE city's complicated terrain, parks in San Francisco tend to have distinct atmospheres. Just as that convoluted landscape shaped and created San Francisco's discrete neighborhoods, it also endows many of its parks with a unique identity. McLaren Park, that sprawling, shaggy open space that spills over the big east–west ridge separating Vistacion Valley from the neighborhoods to the north, has a motley, forgotten natural sublimity. Washington Square was called Il Giardino by the old Italians of North Beach, and its location, in the hinge of a geologic syncline that separates Nob and Telegraph hills, does make it feel like an urban garden. With its raised sides, Alta Plaza is faintly reminiscent of a very elegant sacrificial Aztec mound or that London park where the murder takes place in *Blow-Up*. Lafayette Square, perched atop and flowing down across an unexpected promontory on the edge of Pacific Heights, has a joyous, Raoul Dufy–like quality. Precita Park, tucked oddly in along a built-over stream course at the northern base of Bernal Heights, feels strangely old, as if its uneven ground had been transplanted from some East Coast city. And the granddaddy of the city's parks, Golden Gate, has not one but many atmospheres. The original part of the great park, around the band shell and the conservatory, has a nostalgic, belle epoque

quality; north–south Marx Meadow, the only transverse field in the park, feels as if it's under the special protection of some goddess of feng shui; and the bike trail that runs along Lincoln Way has a wild, Bolinas-like feeling.

These parks all have their charms. But none has the exquisite formality, the Parisian elegance, of Huntington Park. It is a miniature San Francisco version of the Place des Vosges. You expect to see Miss Clavel emerge from adjoining Grace Cathedral with Madeline and the rest of her charges, about to engage in some madcap adventure involving an illicit immersion in the fountain of the tortoises.

The fact that Huntington Park is perched on the vertiginous south shoulder of Nob Hill, just yards away from the virtual cliffs of Mason, Taylor, and Jones streets, certainly contributes to its gemlike ambiance. But just as important, or more so, is its impeccably urbane setting. To the north is elegant Sacramento Street; to the west is soaring Grace Cathedral, much more beautiful than any fake-Gothic cathedral made of poured concrete has a right to be; to the east is a symphony in brownstone, the Flood Mansion; and to the south are the big hotels on California Street, which proudly still wave the banner of Nob Hill opulence. With those majestic surroundings, Huntington Park would have to be a garbage dump not to feel aristocratic.

The park itself is an urban jewel, a symmetrical emerald atop the glittering tiara that is the southern crest of Nob Hill. Lined with acacia trees, boasting two wondrous fountains, a playground, two little lawns, and even a sundial, Huntington Park feels as though it should be off-limits to plebeians. You expect to show up one day and discover that it has turned into New York's Gramercy Park, locked behind a fence to which you do not and will not ever have the key.

The elegant area where Huntington Park now stands, and everything around it, was destroyed in the small hours of the first night of the catastrophe, when the flames that firefighters had been trying desperately to keep to the east jumped Powell Street and consumed everything in their path. The fire destroyed every building on Nob Hill, with a single exception: the Flood Mansion on California Street. That imposing brownstone was heavily damaged, but the walls remained and it was beautifully restored by Willis Polk.

But the Flood Mansion isn't the only reminder of the earthquake and fire. Huntington Park's crowning glory, its superb central fountain, also evokes the 1906 catastrophe—if you know how to look.

## THE FOUNTAIN AND THE FIRE

In 1872, David D. Colton, who made his fortune buying real estate in 1860, built an ornate wooden mansion on the site where Huntington Park now stands. When Colton died, his house was bought by Collis Huntington, one of the so-called Big Four tycoons who made their fortunes by investing in the all-important railroad that would later become the omnipotent Southern Pacific—aka the Octopus. Huntington died in 1900, and his mansion was consumed in the 1906 fire. In 1915, Huntington's widow, Arabella (who had kept things all in the plutocratic family by marrying Huntington's nephew), donated the land to the city for a park. The low granite wall that surrounded the house survived the fire and remains to this day enclosing the park.

But that's not the only reminder of the catastrophe. An odd piece of historical serendipity, which involves phantom dolphins and tangible turtles, also connects Huntington Park, albeit extremely tenuously, with the 1906 catastrophe.

The park's most striking feature is its superb fountain, a copy of Rome's Fontana delle Tartarughe ("Turtle Fountain"). The copy, one of four in the United States, was made in Rome in the early nineteenth century and purchased by the Crocker family for their estate in Hillsborough. When the Hillsborough estate was sold, the Crocker heirs donated the fountain to the city, and it was installed in Huntington Park in 1955.

The original fountain was created in 1582 and installed in the Piazza Mattei, in the heart of Rome's Jewish quarter. Like all fountains in Rome, the Fontana delli Mattei, as it was originally called, was intended to provide drinking water for residents. But low water pressure (the ancient aqueduct that fed the fountain by gravity flowed from a reservoir only sixty-seven feet above sea level) reduced its flow to a trickle. As a result, four of the dolphins that originally spouted water from the fountain's brim were removed and replaced in the mid-seventeenth century with the turtles that now grace it.

The fire that destroyed the Huntington mansion, on the site where the fountain now stands, raged out of control in large part because the aqueducts that provided San Francisco's water were ruptured by the earthquake—a historical parallel mutely evoked by those four bronze turtles.

A final poignant reminder of the fire that burned the opulent mansions on Nob Hill stands not on the hill itself but on the shores of Lloyd Lake in Golden Gate Park. The columns known as the Portals of the Past were all that survived of the Towne mansion, which stood a few yards away from Huntington Park, on the corner of California and Mason. They were donated to the city and placed in the park in 1909.

## SAN FRANCISCO'S UR-TRUMP

The successful 1873 launch of Andrew Hallidie's Clay Street Hill Railroad set off a building frenzy on Nob Hill among the city's often newly minted blue bloods. That year, a magnate named James Ben Ali Haggin built the hill's first mansion on the southeast corner of Washington and Taylor, with its lot extending all the way down to Mason. Haggin's house had no fewer than sixty-one rooms, not counting three conservatories. These rooms were not small, either: a parlor was thirty-four by twenty-seven feet, a sitting room twenty-five by eighteen, a dining room thirty-five by twenty-one, and a library twenty-four by twenty-one. But compared with the palaces that followed it, Haggin's ninety-foot-square, fifty-foot-high house was actually the soul of architectural restraint. A critic noted that the Italianate Victorian evinced "no extravagance in column or balustrade, [while] on the other hand there is nothing severely plain. A happy medium has been struck between lavish ornament and niggardly simplicity."

Haggin's pile may have been the last Nob Hill mansion to eschew extravagance in column or balustrade, or even pretend to get anywhere near niggardly simplicity. The overwhelming majority of San Francisco's plutocrats lived in what Rudyard Kipling, who visited the city in 1889, called "aggressive luxury." And nowhere was that in-your-face status flaunting more egregious than on California Street. As discussed in Chapter One, Nob Hill's grand boulevard, which got its own (still-operating) cable car line in 1878, quickly became the architectural bling capital of the world, with one outrageously tricked-out wooden mansion lined up after the next.

In the days before skyscrapers, these baroque palaces were clearly visible for miles. From the crowded downtown streets around Union Square, and the hardscrabble working-class district known as South of the Slot (south of Market Street), draymen and saloonkeepers and factory girls and clerks could look up and see the battlements of their betters looming far above them.

Today, such ostentatious displays of wealth seem to inspire aspiration, not bitterness or resentment—a fact that helped fuel the rise of a certain orange-haired tycoon. But that reaction was less common in the nineteenth century, when class distinctions were sharper. In the dark decade of the 1870s, unemployment was rampant in San Francisco and across the country. Out-of-work men were already angry at the capitalists who owned the mansions on Nob Hill, and the fact that

those plutocrats hired cheap Chinese workers goaded them beyond endurance. For these bitter men in the city's lower depths, the peacock palaces on California Street became hated symbols of a system they were convinced was rigged against them.

An opportunistic rabble-rouser named Denis Kearney seized the moment. Kearney was the best known of the "sand lot orators," so called because they delivered their harangues to crowds of men who gathered at the sand lots near City Hall. With his gift for appealing to mass resentment and his peculiar mixed ideology, equal parts antielitist populism and racism, Kearney bore more than a passing resemblance to the aforementioned orange-haired real estate developer turned president of the United States. Originally a small-business owner, Kearney suddenly switched class allegiances and became a virulent critic of capitalist fat cats and their low-paid Chinese "slaves."

Day after day, Kearney would whip his audience in the sand lots into a frenzy, shouting invective at the "miserable felonius bank-smashers" who used their Chinese pawns, "moon-faced lepers," to steal jobs from Americans. One fall day in 1877, he decided to lead his followers on a march. His target: the mansions on Nob Hill.

## THE PITCHFORK POPULIST
## STORMS THE HEIGHTS

On October 29, 1877, after an especially incendiary speech, Kearney led three thousand shouting men up Nob Hill. Along the way, they burned a Chinese laundry and attacked and beat several Chinese they encountered on the street. Then they headed for Charles Crocker's mansion at California and Taylor.

Charles Crocker was such a perfect target for Kearney that if he had not existed, Kearney might have invented him. One of the so-called Big Four, a quartet of businessmen who made their vast fortunes in the Central Pacific Railroad, Crocker had erected a vast, garish Second Empire–style monument to his engorged bank account, complete with a seventy-six-foot tower with a mansard roof and widow's walk from which Crocker could gaze down in Ayn Rand–like superiority upon the little people below.

This mansion fell within the wide scope of Ambrose Bierce's dislikes. "Bitter" Bierce wrote, "There are uglier buildings in America than the Crocker house on Nob Hill; however, they were built with public money for a public purpose; among architectural triumphs of private fortune and personal taste it is peerless."

Not content with his unassuming 12,500-square-foot house, Crocker was determined to buy up the entire block. However, he was thwarted by a German undertaker named Yung, who refused to sell his small house and lot. In retaliation, the railroad magnate surrounded Yung's cottage on three sides with a thirty-foot-high fence (planning codes, Nextdoor, and other forms of recourse to such neighborly villainy did not yet exist), blocking out most of the sun.

Kearney thundered to the mob that Crocker's "spite fence" was proof of the villainy of the plutocrats and warned that if Crocker did not tear it down, he and his followers would give him "the worst beating with the sticks a man ever had . . . If I give an order to hang Crocker, it will be done!"

Kearney then led the mob down California Street toward another ridiculously ostentatious mansion, Leland Stanford's vast pile near Powell Street. But in yet another remarkable parallel with Donald Trump, Kearney and his followers turned out to be much better at attacking the helpless Chinese than at taking on San Francisco capitalists, who had the city's authorities and police force behind them. When he arrived at Stanford's mansion, Kearney simply engaged in more windy fulminations before he and his followers drifted away. Hilariously, sort of, Kearney later became a successful businessman and investor.

Kearney's Workingmen's Party attracted the attention of no less formidable

a critic of capitalism than Karl Marx. But, like Kearney himself, it had no coherent ideology and soon faded away. The wooden symbols of excess on California Street that so incensed Kearney and his followers lasted only a little longer. All the mansions except James Flood's brownstone—now the home of the ultraexclusive, unfortunately acronymed Pacific Union Club—were destroyed in the 1906 fire. Crocker's spite fence stood until 1904, when Yung's children finally sold the parcel to the Crockers. They got to enjoy their ownership of the entire block for only two years. Robber baron row's heyday had lasted a mere thirty years.

After the fire, Nob Hill was never quite as patrician. There are still plenty of rich people in the area—some egregiously face-lifted, fur-wearing women with tightly pulled-back hair, pearl earrings, and frozen countenances turn out every year at the lovely Christmas tree–lighting ceremony in Huntington Park—but it's no longer their main haunt. They live in Pacific Heights, or Presidio Heights, or Seacliff, or—with the rise of tech moguls in their twenties and thirties—in Bernal Heights or Dolores Heights or the Mission. And they keep a much lower profile. No more coaches with liveried footmen carry gouty captains of industry down California Street.

In an 1882 piece on how high society had moved from one neighborhood to the next, the *Chronicle* philosophically mused that Nob Hill, too, might someday cease to be the haunt of the fashionable. "The grand climacteric [on Nob Hill] has not, however, been reached, for the residences of Senator Fair and J. C. Flood have yet to be built," the author wrote. "When those establishments shall have capped the most aristocratic eminence in San Francisco, no further glory can be achieved by the neighborhood. It may then be in order for the nomadic society of our city to emigrate to Bernal Heights, and leave Nob Hill to the lodging house keepers and beer saloons that follow in the wake of retreating fashion."

The piece invoked Bernal Heights as a joke: the idea that the beau monde would ever leave Nob Hill and move out to that remote cow town was absurd. How surprised the author would be to know that 120 years later, his tongue-in-cheek "prediction" would come true.

# CHAPTER 9

# THE MUSIC CONCOURSE

## THE TEMPLE OF MUSIC

THE NATURAL SPLENDORS of Golden Gate Park are so intoxicating that it's easy to overlook the fact that it is a historical time capsule. More than anywhere else in the city, the park, especially its old, eastern part, is a living museum of the belle epoque. In the rest of the city, there are few reminders of the Gilded Age except for Victorian houses. The park, by contrast, has remained largely the same as it was when it was first laid out in 1870. It's filled with artifacts of what Evelyn Wells in her amusing 1939 eponymous romp called San Francisco's "champagne days," from the Conservatory of Flowers to the Alvord Lake Bridge to the Sharon Building to the Francis Scott Key monument to the Japanese Tea Garden. Because their surroundings are unspoiled, these survivors evoke that fabled era with singular power.

And no place conjures up the fin de siècle more than the band shell—or the Spreckels Temple of Music, to give it its suitably overstuffed, gouty name. In part, that's because band shells are relics of a bygone age, when military-style bands were so popular that thousands of people would flock to the Music Concourse on Sunday to hear them. But it's also because it's such an over-the-top piece of architecture—at eighty feet high, it's said to be one of the largest band shells in the Western Hemisphere, a claim that becomes more unimpressive the more you

think about it. It's undeniably impressive, but it almost looks more like a cheesy architectural detail blown up to monstrous size than a functional structure; it's at once wondrous and corny. You expect Professor Harold Hill, in full gold-braided, seventy-six-trombones-leading glory, to come high-stepping around its colonnade.

People in the nineteenth century did not feel the way about band shells the way we do now, for the Spreckels Temple of Music was actually the third one in the park. The first was built in 1882, followed by a larger one in 1888. In 1894, the former leader of the Vienna Prater Orchestra, Fritz Scheel, was hired to direct the Golden Gate Park Band on Sundays. Scheel's musicianship received high praise, but he appears to have been one of the most linguistically challenged individuals in San Francisco history. According to Raymond Clary in *The Making of Golden Gate Park: The Early Years 1865–1906*, although Scheel had lived in the United States for two years, he knew only two words of English—"the same." But Scheel's faulty grasp of his adopted tongue does not seem to have been his biggest problem. According to an *Examiner* reporter, Scheel also knew only one word of German—"gesundheit." It is not clear what, if any, language Scheel was proficient in.

Undeterred by the fact that the leader of the Golden Gate Park band acknowledged applause only by saying "The same!" or, when he was really feeling it, "Gesundheit!" large numbers of San Franciscans flocked to hear his band. In 1895, discussions began about building a larger band shell. Adolph Bernard, president of the park commission, convinced his father, sugar magnate Claus Spreckels, to pay for it. Spreckels gave $75,000 of the $79,000 it cost to build the grand new structure. The Reid Brothers architects, who also designed San Francisco's first skyscraper, the Call Building, and the Fairmont Hotel, designed the classical structure, faced in Colusa sandstone and with an acoustically reflective coffered shell.

On Admission Day, September 9, 1900, a crowd estimated at between thirty thousand and one hundred thousand people filled what was then called Concert Valley for the dedication of the Spreckels Temple of Music. The *Chronicle* reported that "every seat in the immense tree-shaded basin before the temple had its occupant; almost as far as the eye could reach was a sea of faces; but the concourse was not so vast but that the music reached to the farthermost limit and beyond, for the big sandstone sounding board before which the band played sent the melodies outside the grounds to the cars that were still parkward bound."

When Spreckels addressed the huge crowd, he said he had made the gift in gratitude for the benefits California had conferred upon him as an immigrant. He had chosen to build a bandstand because music was universally uplifting, and he was determined that it should be "rendered free to all and under circumstances that would make it attractive to rich and poor alike."

Spreckels explained why he chose to place the temple in Golden Gate Park: "It already ranks among the finest parks in the world. It is the resort of thousands. It is the playground of the children, the festal garden of youths and maidens, the recreation of the worker, the solitude of the thinker, the parade of wealth and fashion, the object lesson of artists, and in many ways it ministers to the studies of men of science. Here, then, where all gather, it is proper that the music which charms them should be provided with a stately and noble pavilion."

Spreckels's words reflect the immense pride San Franciscans took, and the love they felt, for their great park at a time when city parks were still fairly new. Just half a century before Spreckels spoke, there were no city parks in the United States, no places where all the citizens of a city, rich and poor, could go to find trees, and lawns, and music, and open air. And although his language may be a little purple and dated, the sentiments behind his speech—and the democratic vistas they evoke—remain true today.

# THE MIDWINTER FAIR

The Music Concourse in Golden Gate Park is a remnant of the first and least-known of San Francisco's three world fairs: the 1894 California Midwinter International Exposition. The Midwinter Fair, as it was usually called, was the brainchild of *San Francisco Chronicle* publisher M. H. de Young, who wanted to promote California and demonstrate that San Francisco was a world-class city.

San Francisco's image needed some polishing. The former Gold Rush frontier town had grown to be a bustling city of three hundred thousand, but during the Gilded Age, the gulf between the nabobs in their ludicrous mansions on Nob Hill and the workers in the lower depths had become a chasm. Vicious tong warfare in Chinatown and the depraved sexual license of the Barbary Coast were also civic black eyes.

De Young also hoped to jump-start San Francisco's economy. During the national depression known as the Panic of 1893, the city had hit hard times: unemployment hit 10 percent and stayed there for five years, a situation not repeated until the Great Depression.

By starting the fair in winter, de Young intended to draw attention to the fact that California had a much better winter climate than the East Coast. He pushed for the privately financed fair to be held in Golden Gate Park. Legendary park superintendent John McLaren, the tenacious Scot who ran the park for a mind-boggling fifty-three years, was bitterly opposed to the idea, fearing it would damage his park's lawns, flowers, and trees, but he was overridden. When another park official complained that it would take a hundred years to replace the trees that would be cut down for the fair, de Young retorted, "What is a tree? What are a thousand trees compared to the benefits of the exposition?" (California gubernatorial candidate Ronald Reagan was later to utter a similar sentiment when he said, "A tree is a tree—how many more do you need to look at?")

The landscape plan of the 160-acre fair was designed by civil engineer Michael O'Shaughnessy, who was later to break John Muir's heart by damming Hetch Hetchy valley to create San Francisco's water supply. At its heart was the Grand Court of Honor, located on the site of the present-day Music Concourse, which was called Concert Valley at the time. The Court of Honor was a nine-acre sunken oval, carved out of the sand dunes by horse-drawn sleds. Its centerpiece was a 272-foot electric tower that boasted what was supposedly the most powerful searchlight in the world, so bright that boosters made the dubious claim that you could read a newspaper by its beam at a distance of eight miles. Three different viewing platforms, including the Belvista Café on the second level, afforded fairgoers a panoramic view of the fair and the park.

Located around the electric tower were the five principal buildings of the fair, ornate piles built in an eccentric mix of architectural styles. The Fine Arts Building was particularly odd: a squat Egyptian-style building surmounted by a pyramid, it looked ominously like a gigantic mausoleum. Nonetheless, it was the only large building not to be torn down at the end of the fair, becoming the first iteration of the de Young Museum.

The Midwinter Fair was inspired by Chicago's 1893 Columbian Exposition, which boasted a raucous entertainment section called the Midway Plaisance (remember that name). San Francisco's fair featured popular entertainments such as a Firth wheel, the counterpart of Chicago's Ferris wheel, and a fright ride called Dante's Inferno, which riders entered through a huge dragon's mouth. There was also the '49 Mining Camp, which boasted gambling tables, a saloon, and a daily stagecoach robbery, thus turning a history only forty-five years old into profitable myth—more or less what the city did ad nauseam on the 50th anniversary of the Summer of Love. (San Francisco's next world's fair, the 1915 Panama-Pacific

International Exposition, also featured a '49 Camp, but one that was so authentic it had be closed down—a story told in the next chapter.)

The oddest and—to our modern sensibilities—creepiest entertainments at the fair were its ethnic exhibitions, which possessed all the cultural sensitivity the late nineteenth century was noted for. These included an Esquimaux Village with igloos made of papier-mâché and an artificial lake on which fairgoers could gawk at real Eskimos paddling around in kayaks; an Oriental Village featuring Cairo Street, boasting scimitar-wielding men and a curvaceous belly dancer named Little Egypt; and the Dahomey Village, where paying customers could eye muscular African tribesmen and ogle bare-breasted women. The latter exhibition was noteworthy for a particularly egregious bit of ethnic deception, one that today would be unthinkable but made a little-known but major contribution to American culture.

## THE DAHOMEY VILLAGE AND BERT WILLIAMS

Like a number of other exhibitions at the Midwinter Fair, the Dahomey Village was a rerun from Chicago's Columbian Exposition. At the White City, as the 1893 World's Fair was called with unintentional irony, it was part of a vast anthropological treasure trove intended to introduce fairgoers to exotic cultures and to the new field of anthropology. In an astonishingly ambitious undertaking, a team of three anthropologists—including the young Franz Boas—dispatched one hundred explorers to go to fifty countries around the world and collect the most interesting artifacts they could find.

The collecting expedition was actually more scientifically rigorous and culturally sensitive than others at the time. However, the collectors engaged in one practice that would be unthinkable today. They not only brought home artifacts but took home entire groups of native people and the villages they lived in. No fewer than three thousand indigenous people were shipped to the fair, including the aforementioned Eskimos and Egyptians, but also North and South American Indians, Laplanders, Maoris, Javanese, Melanesians—and sixty-nine Dahomeyan villagers, along with thirty of their houses.

The Kingdom of Dahomey fascinated Westerners because it was seen as particularly exotic. Its king had recently led his people in a fierce losing fight against French colonizers; it was the last major port of call for slave ships making the Middle Passage; and it practiced large-scale human sacrifice and cannibalism.

The anthropologists wanted the villages to be presented along the fair's Midway Plaisance as a dignified row of world cultures, but fair directors, anxious for the fair to turn a profit, handed control of the midway over to a protégé of P. T. Barnum's, who turned the strip into a downmarket carnival-like venue, squeezing the "native villages" next to beer halls, thrill rides, and hootchy-kootchy girls.

The Midway Plaisance and the ethnic villages were a big hit. Midwinter Fair organizers arranged for several of them, including the Dahomeyans, the Cairo Village, and the Eskimos, to be shipped to San Francisco when the Columbian Exposition ended.

At this point, a completely different character enters the story. He's only a historical footnote to the fair, but some footnotes are more interesting than the text above them.

In the early 1890s, a young black comic actor named Bert Williams arrived in San Francisco and began trying to find work. Williams had been born in the Bahamas and moved as a child to Riverside, where he first began performing. In San Francisco, Williams met another young black comedian named George Walker, and the two men began working at a minstrel show called Martin and Selig's Mastodon Minstrels. They also began performing as a two-man act, Williams and Walker, at a Market Street dive called Jack Halahan's Cramorne

Theater (later, by weird coincidence, renamed the Midway Plaisance), which the *San Francisco Daily Times* called a "sad bad old 'dump.'"

While they were grinding through their comedy routines at the dump on Market Street, the Midwinter Fair opened. The Dahomey Village on the Midway Plaisance was supposed to open its doors, but the ship carrying the actual Dahomeyans had not arrived. Desperate, the exhibition's producers went out and hired local blacks to impersonate Dahomeyan villagers. Two of the men they hired were Williams and Walker.

The real Africans arrived a few months later, and the two young comedians and the other ringers were let go. But as Walker later wrote, "Having free access to the Fair grounds, we were permitted to visit the natives from Africa. It was there, for the first time, that we were brought in close touch with native Africans, and the study of these natives interested us very much. We were not long in deciding that if we ever reached the point of having a show of our own, we would delineate and feature native African characters as far as we could, and still remain Americans, and make our acting interesting and entertaining to American audiences."

Williams and Walker made good on their intentions. In 1903, they used their knowledge of the Dahomeyans when they starred in a musical called *In Dahomey*, one of the first black musicals to open on Broadway. Williams went on to become the first black performer to have a starring role on Broadway and the bestselling black recording artist before 1920.

Williams and Walker were not only tremendously successful, they were racial pioneers. In their subtlety and humanity, the characters Williams and Walker played went beyond the crude racist stereotypes that had hitherto constrained black performers. Walker asserted that their knowledge of Africans was partly responsible: "I have no hesitation in stating that the departure from what was popularly known as the American 'darky' ragtime limitations to native African characteristics has helped to greatly increase the value of the black performer on the American Stage."

History, T.S. Eliot said, has many cunning passageways and contrived corridors, but few can be as unlikely, and ironic, as the story of Bert Williams and the Dahomey Village. If a weird African anthropological spectacle at a world's fair in 1894 San Francisco had not needed some American ringers, two young men would never have gained the cultural knowledge that helped them change the history of black performance in the United States.

# CHAPTER 10

# THE PALACE OF FINE ARTS

## CURATING THE PLANET

THE PALACE OF Fine Arts, one of San Francisco's strangest and most beautiful buildings, is the only surviving structure from the second and grandest of the city's world fairs, the 1915 Panama-Pacific International Exposition. The PPIE was intended to serve two functions: to commemorate the completion of the Panama Canal and to announce to the world that San Francisco had come through the 1906 earthquake better than ever. These Chamber of Commerce–type goals were more than achieved by the exposition's vast ambition—and swamped by its sheer craziness. Equal parts kitsch and Dionysus, it was a wild architectural acid trip, an ur-Disneyland whose fantastical buildings, dazzling lighting effects, and Saturnalian atmosphere anticipated another mind-blowing temporary city dreamed up in San Francisco, Burning Man.

The exposition's modest goal was to "curate the planet"—to offer "a microcosm so nearly complete that if all the world were destroyed except the 635 acres of land within the Exposition gates, the material basis of the life of today could have been reproduced from the exemplifications of the arts, inventions and industries there exhibited," as the official history put it.

The heart of the PPIE was the dazzling Jewel City, made up of dozens of

phantasmagoric buildings, monumental courts, gushing fountains, and extravagant sculptures, which variously paid homage to Athens, Rome, Byzantium, Paris, and Cordoba, with the whole lit by an avant-garde lighting system bearing the panopticon-like name the Total Illumination Plan. The fair's centerpiece was the 435-foot-high Tower of Jewels, a wedding cake–shaped structure covered with 102,000 colored-glass artificial jewels called Novagems, which hung on hooks and swung in the breeze. From there fairgoers could sate their architectural appetites at the Court of Abundance, originally called the Court of the Ages, a 340-foot-square courtyard featuring sunken gardens, a central pool, and a fountain and ornamented with sculptured lobsters, crabs, tortoises, and other examples of what some hungry observer dubbed "seafood gothic." A tower at the north end resembled a two-hundred-foot altar. The ensemble drew on a wild grab bag of sources, including Portuguese Gothic, French, Moorish, Romanesque, Oriental, and Hindu. The overall effect was described as a "sermon in stone."

Like Chicago's 1893 Columbian Exposition, the PPIE had a large section that catered to earthier tastes. This mile-long midway, called the Joy Zone, was packed with outrageously kitschy facades, restaurants, and an assortment of rides, historic re-creations, and other entertainments. As the official fair historian Frank Morton Todd described it: "It was a great amusement street, and with its Golden Buddha, its tall suffragette and twin soldiers wonderful before Toyland, its Chinese pagoda, the giant holding back the waters of the Dayton flood . . . its cliffs and crags of the Grand Canyon, and of Yellowstone, and particularly of the 'Submarines' with Neptune and his rearing sea horses, the square tower of Blarney Castle lifting above the 'Shamrock Isle' . . . the whole scene had a grand and imposing aspect in spite of its necessary garishness."

The zany facades of the buildings on the Joy Zone helped spur the vernacular movement in architecture, which was about to find its dream habitat in Southern California, aka the Land of Necessary Garishness. All those hot-dog stands in the shape of wieners and diners that look like flying saucers had their origins at the PPIE.

The Joy Zone featured more than 250 attractions, including a five-acre reproduction of the Panama Canal, a giant "cyclorama" of the Battle of Gettysburg, a depiction of the battle between the *Monitor* and the *Merrimack*, and a re-creation of the Dayton Flood (which proved, like many of the concessions, to be a major money loser).

The zone's most outrageous attraction was the '49 Camp, which in addition to staged shoot-outs and bronco-busting displays featured actual booze, actual gambling, and actual prostitutes. The authorities repeatedly closed it, but the Days of '49 Company managed to keep the booze flowing, the faro games going, and the "soiled doves" working the johns. After the third closure, fair poo-bahs had had enough and revoked its license. But the attraction that took its place, rebranded Pioneer Days, featured such blatantly open (and illegal) gambling that it, too, was closed down after less than two months. The forty-niners, the city's sacred founding fathers, proved to be as unruly in re-creation as they were in real life. (A classic piece of San Francisco doggerel is too irresistible not to repeat here: "The miners came in '49/The whores in '51./And when they got together/They produced the Native Son.")

Equally controversial, and equally hard to shut down, was a show called *Underground Chinatown*, which was produced by theater owner Sid Grauman, later to open the famous Chinese Theatre in Hollywood. Held, naturally, in a basement, *Underground Chinatown* played off Chinatown's reputation for vice, which had long drawn tourists eager to behold these unspeakably exotic sins with their own eyes. *Underground Chinatown* featured a den peopled with wax opium smokers and, most offensively, a scene in which a white woman was forced into sexual slavery by a Chinese drug lord. After Chinese officials angrily protested,

exposition officials shut down the concession. However, the wily Grauman reopened it two months later, changing its name to *Underground Slumming*, removing the Chinese characters, and billing it as a morality play about the dangers of drugs. These cosmetic alterations made it impossible for the Chinese to object to it, but references to "opium dens" and "slave girls" made it all too obvious what the show was actually about.

But such tawdry attractions were outnumbered by the countless fair exhibitions dedicated to edification and uplift. The sixty-five thousand people a day who flooded into the Jewel City during its 288-day run—its total attendance was nineteen million—could marvel at an exhibit of never-before-seen color photography, learn about the quattrocento by visiting seven buildings designed in different Italian Renaissance styles, make a transcontinental telephone call, and sit on the keys of a giant Underwood typewriter.

They could also view a large collection of contemporary paintings and sculpture, which was displayed at the most original and poetic of the fair's ephemeral buildings—the Palace of Fine Arts. Located at the opposite end of the fairgrounds from the crowded, frenetic Joy Zone, the Palace of Fine Arts was also its spiritual opposite: it was haunting, evocative, and otherworldly. Fairgoers fell in love with the great, enigmatic ruined temple on its beautiful lagoon—in fact, it was so popular that a movement to save it started when the fair was still underway. To this day, the Palace of Fine Arts is one of the most beloved buildings in San Francisco.

But this masterpiece had a very odd birth. In fact, the great architect who designed it got the commission only because of an unusual act of generosity on the part of a notoriously egotistical colleague.

## THE FREE SPIRIT

Bernard Maybeck, the architect who designed the Palace of Fine Arts, was a free spirit. He wore handmade clothing, didn't care about making money (he had his wife, Annie, bill his clients), did not schmooze or network, and generally comported himself like an absentminded professor. As a result, most of his colleagues didn't take him seriously. He was commonly referred to as a freak.

In 1910, Maybeck created his masterpiece, the First Church of Christ, Scientist, in the town where he lived, Berkeley. Despite this towering achievement and many other superb buildings, when the architectural advisory committee for the Panama-Pacific International Exposition was named in 1912, he was passed over, although many of his colleagues and some of his students were chosen. This enraged Annie, "his little fighting tiger," who assailed the committee with letters until Maybeck was given the job of coordinating design work in the Joy Zone.

The commission to design the Palace of Fine Arts, one of the most important buildings in the fair, went to Willis Polk, the famous—and famously volatile—architect who was head of the architectural committee. But Polk was put off by what looked like an inferior site, a watery bog on the west end of the fair's grounds, and he was also consumed by his bureaucratic responsibilities. Polk was so flummoxed by the assignment that he hired Maybeck—nominally as a draftsman, but in reality to come up with a design. Maybeck worked over a weekend and came up with a charcoal drawing. He rolled it out on Polk's desk and said, "This thing you call a mudhole, that's your opportunity—you can make a reflecting mirror of that."

In Maybeck's sketch, the muddy bog had become a crystalline lagoon, above which towered a majestic domed rotunda, with a long, curving colonnade flanking it along the water. The architectural advisory committee loved the sketch and congratulated Polk. But the notoriously egotistical architect surprised his colleagues by saying it was not his design, but Maybeck's, and Maybeck should be hired to finish it. The rest is architectural history.

## THE FOLLY

The Palace of Fine Arts is so august and feels so timeless that it's easy to forget it's really just an enormous folly. That weird and wonderful architectural genre is difficult to define, but it is characterized by structures whose decorative functions outweigh their practical ones. The folly is typically an excessive or fantastical take on an ancient building form, such as a Greek or Roman temple, a Chinese pagoda, a Tatar tent, or an Egyptian pyramid. Occupying an aesthetic no-man's-land somewhere between conventional architecture and a stage set, follies are built for pleasure, but they can also be deeply serious, in the same way that stage sets can be serious. Like the metaphysical paintings of de Chirico, with their haunted arcades and cosmically empty squares, they are suffused with loss, otherworldliness, mystery. Yet there is also something childlike about them. They are an intoxicating combination of darkness and playfulness.

To appreciate the unique achievement of the Palace of Fine Arts, it's useful to compare it with another great folly, the Broken Column in the Désert de Retz, an eighteenth-century French folly garden considered the finest in the world. Of the

original seventeen or twenty structures in the Désert de Retz, ten are still extant. The most noteworthy of these is the Broken Column, a mighty piece of a vast, ruined, imaginary temple that also functions as a house.

The difference between these two pseudoclassic temples is summed up by one of the essential formulations of antiquity, Aristotle's definition of tragedy as evoking pity and terror. The Broken Column evokes terror, the Palace of Fine Arts pity. As Diana Ketcham writes in *Le Désert de Retz*, the Broken Column "stands like a solitary beacon, signaling the visitor to prepare for an encounter with the bizarre." Because the viewer is intended to see it as only a small fragment of a lost temple of monstrous size, its scale is terrifying: "The viewer [is] reduced, rendered small and bewildered before the mysterious bulk of the Broken Column." The Broken Column is like a fantasy set: it recalls the famous last shot in *Planet of the Apes*, when a camera slowly pulls back to reveal that a large shape in the foreground is actually the Statue of Liberty, half-buried in the sand at the edge of the sea. The past that it evokes is alien and unknowable, like the gigantic Assyrian gates in the British Museum or the ruined temples at Karnak.

The Palace of Fine Arts, by contrast, is peaceful and dreamlike. Its sublimity is reassuring, not frightening. Maybeck endowed his temple and its setting with these benign qualities because he intended it to serve a very specific function at the fair. He saw the building and the lagoon as a kind of aesthetic passageway, or buffer, between the chaotic fairgrounds and what he called the "melancholy-inducing experience" of viewing the art in the large building behind the colonnades. Art was a "sad and serious matter," he said in a lecture, but beauty could temper it. The palace's purpose was to create a mood of "sadness modified by the feeling that beauty has a soothing influence."

## THE DREAM PALACE

To realize his vision, Maybeck rummaged through an eclectic collection of historic buildings and works of art. "The process is similar to that of matching the color of ribbons," he wrote. "You pick up a blue ribbon, hold it alongside the sample in your hand, and at a glance you know it matches or it does not. You do the same with architecture; you examine a historic form and see whether the effect it produces on your mind matches the feeling you are trying to portray." For Maybeck, the most important of those historic forms was what he described as "an old Roman ruin, away from civilization, which two thousand years before was the center of action and full of life, and now is partly overgrown with bushes and trees—such ruins give the mind a sense of sadness." He was particularly inspired by the eighteenth-century Italian artist Giovanni Piranesi's etchings of ancient Roman ruins, especially the foliage-covered ruin of the Temple of Minerva Medica.

However, Maybeck also drew inspiration from two paintings that share some of the ominous and disturbing qualities of dark follies, like the Broken Column in the Désert de Retz. He was fascinated by the famous painting *Isle of the Dead* by the Swiss symbolist painter Arnold Böcklin, and he was also inspired by a more obscure painting he saw in Munich, which depicted a "princess sitting on a throne who, in a mad fit, ordered freezing water to be thrown over nude maidens, amid snow and icicles." This figure was Countess Erzsébet Báthory, a notorious Hungarian noblewoman who is said to have been the most prolific female serial killer in history, torturing and killing as many as 650 women and girls between 1590 and 1609. (It is probably just as well that this singularly creepy source of inspiration for one of San Francisco's most beloved buildings is not well-known.)

Maybeck took the comforting aspects from these sublime paintings and left out the disturbing ones. In a book he published about the Palace of Fine Arts, Maybeck wrote that Böcklin's painting was too sad to serve as a frontispiece to the art galleries, just as a Greek temple on a wild island surrounded by churning seas would be too terrifying—too much, we might add, like the Broken Column in the Désert de Retz. To hit the necessary note, Maybeck set his temple in a peaceful lagoon, which he believed would give the feeling of a comforting maternal embrace and achieve a "transition from sadness to content." He regarded the lagoon as the most important part of his design.

Like the Broken Column, Maybeck's folly evokes the sadness of the past but does so in a profoundly affirmative way, one that folds that sadness back into the living human world. As a result, the Palace of Fine Arts transcends its status as a folly in a way that the Broken Column does not. The Broken Column is a stunning science-fiction set; the Palace of Fine Arts is something larger and deeper.

The palace alone was spared the fate of the other fair buildings, almost all of which were destroyed (a handful were shipped elsewhere). But like those other buildings, the Palace of Fine Arts was not intended to last. When it inevitably started to fall apart, Maybeck initially did not want it preserved. "I think the main building should be torn down and redwoods planted around—completely around—the rotunda," he wrote. "As they grow, the columns would slowly crumble at the same speed. Then I would like to design an altar, with the figure of a maiden praying, to install in the grove of redwoods . . . I should like my palace to die behind those great trees of its own accord, and become its own cemetery." But Maybeck came to support the movement to preserve the palace. It was completely rebuilt in 1965.

Maybeck memorably called himself a "long-distance dreamer." In 1923, when he was sixty-one, he wrote, "There is something bigger and more worthwhile than the things we see about us, the things we live by and strive for. There is an undiscovered beauty, a divine excellence, just beyond us. Let us stand on tiptoe, forgetting the nearer things and grasp what we may."

Maybeck's long-distance dreaming transformed what on its face is a fake temple, a folly inspired by a hodgepodge of historical material, into a real temple. It is a dream palace in two senses: Maybeck dreamed it up, and it inspires dreams among all those who see it. It is a shrine to beauty that even nonbelievers can believe in.

## STRAWBERRY ISLAND FOREVER

The area where the Palace of Fine Arts now stands has a history as evocative as the great folly itself and as eclectic as the exposition of which Maybeck's building is the last reminder. This little stretch of the city's northern waterfront was successively a bucolic island, the city's first bathing resort, an industrial zone, and a refugee camp.

The site of the Palace of Fine Arts was once a saltwater marsh on the edge of a tidal slough, one of the three largest wetland areas in San Francisco (the other two were Mission Bay and Islais Marsh to the south). Its marshes and convoluted waterways extended almost as far east as what is now Fillmore Street and almost as far west as today's Warming Hut on the walkway to the Golden Gate Bridge. In 1942, William R. P. Clark recalled, "The writer on one occasion went in a row boat through these waterways nearly to the western end of the present Letterman General Hospital."

The most intriguing feature of this stretch of the northern waterfront was a large, curving sandy spit known as Strawberry Island or Sand Point. Strawberry Island is clearly visible in nineteenth-century photographs of the area. About the size of fifteen square city blocks, it extended out into the bay between what is now the eastern end of the Crissy Field Marsh to present-day Pierce and Francisco streets. The Palace of Fine Arts stands on the northern end of the tidal slough and wetlands that separated Strawberry Island from the mainland. Actually, it was an island only at high tide; at low tide you could walk across a narrow beach at its western end to the mainland. The sandy spit derived its name because wild strawberries grew on it.

Those wild strawberries surely attracted San Francisco's first residents, the Yelamu Indians, who had a seasonal village called Petlenuc just east of the present-day Crissy Field Marsh, close to the western end of Strawberry Island. The several hundred Yelamu who lived in San Francisco knew where all the edible plants on the sandy peninsula were: they told the Spanish about another wild strawberry patch near Lands End, where a famous *merienda* (picnic) was held at the end of the charmed dozen years when the tiny hamlet of Yerba Buena was under Mexican rule. It's even possible to conjecture that the proximity of the wild strawberries may have been part of the reason the Yelamu set up camp nearby.

Little did San Francisco's indigenous inhabitants know that after they had been driven out of their home, the last of their conquerors would erect various Indian-themed tourist attractions, including a faux "pueblo" erected on top of the entry building of the Grand Canyon of Arizona concession, just a few hundred yards to the east of the place where they once gathered wild strawberries on an empty beach.

# HARBOR VIEW

In 1864, when San Francisco had a population of about sixty thousand and the idea of a world's fair would have seemed preposterous, Strawberry Island and the waterfront near it was the home of one of the city's first bathing and pleasure resorts, Harbor View Baths.

Harbor View Baths was created by a German immigrant named Rudolph Herman. After arriving in San Francisco in 1854, Herman first opened a bathhouse on Black Point Cove (today's Aquatic Park) in 1860. He moved to a sparsely populated area around a popular roadhouse called the Presidio House, near the present-day intersection of Lyon and Lombard. In 1862, he acquired Strawberry Island and lands nearby and began building roads, landscaping the grounds, and erecting a building he called the Harbor View House. In 1864, he opened Harbor View Baths. Over the years, Herman enlarged the resort, sinking $60,000 into it by 1892.

The main attraction of Herman's resort was its hot- and cold-water baths, featuring hot salt water heated in zinc tubs as well as cold saltwater baths. Guests had access to thirty-three separate bathing apartments with suits and towels, "under constant supervision" of an attendant. The resort also had a large sandy beach for guests who preferred surf bathing, two wharves, and several boats and launches.

Just as big a draw for San Franciscans starved for greenery—the city had almost no verdant areas until Golden Gate Park opened in the 1870s—were the resort's grounds. Its large hotel was surrounded by three blocks of lush, landscaped grounds, described in an 1884 guidebook as "a perfect fairy land of green lawns, pleasant walks, arbors and drives, shaded by handsome groves of monterey cypress, pine, acacia, blue gum, pepper and other evergreens." For ten cents, visitors to Harbor View Park, as it became known, could enjoy garden concerts, boat racing, prize swimming, and a shooting range. Orchestral and band music and dancing was offered beneath the 130-square-foot dance hall called the Pavilion, whose roof was supported by a single central pillar and boasted "a dancing floor unsurpassed on the coast." Diners enjoyed seafood at Louis Swartz's popular restaurant.

Fraternal and ethnic-group organizations, highly popular in the nineteenth century, frequented Harbor View Park. For example, in April 1897, the Swiss Sharpshooters Benevolent Society held their thirty-first annual picnic there for several hundred people.

Early visitors to Harbor View, as the entire neighborhood came to be called,

used one of San Francisco's most romantic, little-known roads, a toll road called the Bay Shore and Fort Point Road. This macadamized road, which opened in 1864, started at Bay and Jones, hugged the shoreline through Black Point (Fort Mason), headed west to Harbor View, and ended at Fort Point. The exposed westernmost section of this road, north of the old tidal slough and wetlands, was so battered by storms, tides, and blowing sand that it had begun to decay by 1867. But the eastern section remained in use until the 1880s.

Harbor View Park was seized by city officials after the 1906 earthquake and converted into a refugee camp. It reopened briefly after the camp was closed in 1907 but closed for good in 1909, when the city decided to incorporate the area into a tax assessment district. In 1913, the city acquired the defunct park and demolished it to make room for the Panama-Pacific International Exposition.

The one remaining feature from the old baths was a stand of cypress trees, which adorned the grounds of the fair's California Hall. But soon they, too, were cut down. With their disappearance, Harbor View Park had vanished as completely as old Strawberry Island, the sandy, tide-swept spit on which it was built.

# THE EARTHQUAKE SHACKS OF HARBOR VIEW

After the April 1906 catastrophe, the second-largest earthquake refugee camp in the city was located at Harbor View Park, just north of the present-day Palace of Fine Arts. Its twenty-five hundred residents initially lived in tents, but by the fall and winter those refugees who still remained in the camps, most of them poor, had moved into several hundred of the 5,610 small earthquake cottages the city constructed to provide homes for working-class San Franciscans.

Thanks to an enlightened relief policy, the cottages were essentially given free to their residents, who had only to buy or lease land (cheap at the time) onto which to move them. After the Harbor View refugee camp closed in 1907, hundreds of earthquake cottages ended up being moved into the Harbor View neighborhood—probably the largest number in any neighborhood in the city.

At the time, Harbor View was not the wealthy enclave it would become after it was developed in the 1920s and 1930s and changed its name to the Marina. Heavy industries, including factories and shipyards, rubbed shoulders with modest stores and other businesses, a few middle-class homes, and lots of working-class housing, including the earthquake shacks. But when the PPIE decided to hold the fair in Harbor View, it needed to clear the whole area—shacks and all.

The Exposition Company, the entity charged with acquiring the land for the PPIE, purchased some of the shacks and sold them to the highest bidder, on the condition they be removed within thirty days of the sale. But the Exposition Company also leaned on the San Francisco Board of Health to have most of the shacks simply condemned. In 1911 and early 1912, no fewer than 415 homes in Harbor View, mostly refugee shacks and other earthquake housing, were condemned as unsanitary. Those not promptly taken down by their owners were torn down. It was a foreshadowing of the city's removal of homeless tent encampments a century later, with one difference: the tent encampments keep coming back.

# CHAPTER 11

# THE ALEMANY HEALTH CENTER

## THE LAST REAL NEIGHBORHOOD
## IN SAN FRANCISCO

FOR MOST SAN Franciscans, the Excelsior is one of the places where their mental map of the city is creased and illegible. They are vaguely aware that it's somewhere out by McLaren Park and marked by a weird turquoise-colored tower, but that's about it. The confusing interweavings of San Jose Avenue, Alemany Boulevard, and Mission Street, along with the Berlin Wall–like Interstate 280 freeway, render everything to their south terra incognita. Even though I was a San Francisco taxi driver for seven years, I never quite figured that part of the city out.

The Excelsior is a pleasantly unpretentious neighborhood, one of the few working-joe quarters left in the city. Although a lot of those working joes and janes now have jobs in tech or finance instead of grocery stores or auto repair shops and paid a million bucks for their houses instead of $25,000—in 2017, the real estate website Redfin named it the second-hottest neighborhood in the city—the Excelsior doesn't feel upscale or trendy, just stolid and solid. There are no destination restaurants or hotshot bakeries, it's one of the most racially diverse parts of town, and there are more cars with 49ers or Warriors banners attached to their aerials per capita than anywhere else in town except for a few holdout,

hairnetted, muscle-shirt-wearing, low-rider-cruising blocks in the Mission. It's the working-class (using a broad definition of that term) equivalent of middle-class West Portal, another frozen-in-amber neighborhood, except without the white picket fences.

The Excelsior may not be glamorous, but it has the most cosmopolitan street names in town. The heart of the neighborhood is traversed by a series of streets named Brazil, Persia, Russia, France, and Italy, which are intersected by (in order as you go south) London, Paris, Lisbon, Madrid, Edinburgh, Naples, Vienna, Athens, Moscow, Munich, Prague, and Dublin. Which means that, yes, you can live on the corner of Paris and France, or Naples and Italy, or Moscow and Russia. For those of a more Arthurian bent, there is also an Avalon Avenue and, naturally, an Excelsior Avenue. Actually, these last two avenues were formerly named Japan and China, and acquired their mystical nomenclature only when the widespread anti-Asian sentiments of the early 20th century led them to be renamed. Just to make sure that South Asia did not sneak away with a street name, India Avenue was also changed to Peru Avenue.

The Excelsior's main stem, Mission Street, is a bit shabby, which might sound like a put-down anywhere other than 2020 San Francisco, when indifferently prepared food, dingy storefronts, and nonexistent marketing plans feel like a desperately needed oasis of mediocrity in a nightmarish desert of unrelentingly excellent cups of $5 coffee. There are few unusual buildings or points of major historic interest here, although Mission Street runs more or less on the route of the most historic road in all of California, El Camino Real (the Royal Road), which the Spanish built to connect Alta California's twenty-one missions. But on the corner of Onondaga and Alemany stand two buildings that not only are architecturally significant but are two of the only reminders of a fascinating and remarkably progressive city program—the Emergency Hospital System.

## THE EMERGENCY HOSPITAL SYSTEM

The Spanish-style building at 45 Onondaga Street, and the smaller structure next door at Number 35, look slightly out of place on their street: their architecture is a little too elegant and unusual. But few passersby realize just how unusual these buildings were. They were part of an innovative city program called the Emergency Hospital System—a free, citywide system that provided emergency medical care to residents in their own neighborhoods, twenty-four hours a day, 365 days a year. At 35 Onondaga was the Alemany Emergency Hospital and at 45 Onondaga the Alemany Health Center, a health clinic. The two facilities opened in 1933 and operated until 1978, when the entire EHS was shut down.

In the days before widespread health insurance and the 911 system, the Emergency Hospital System was a remarkably enlightened public program, dedicated to providing free emergency health care to all, regardless of their ability to pay. Like Franklin D. Roosevelt's New Deal, which kicked in at about the same time, it was both attacked as dangerously communistic and defended as the finest in the country.

The system's origins can be traced to a series of newspaper exposés written by the city's leading muckraker, an intrepid reporter named Winifred Bonfils, who wrote for William Randolph Hearst's *Examiner* under the name Annie Laurie. (See page 63.) The city's first emergency room was located in the basement of the old City Hall. In 1889, Hearst began a campaign to expose how San Francisco's ambulance and emergency services lagged behind those in East Coast cities. In 1896, Laurie collapsed on Market Street, was admitted to the emergency room, and wrote a story revealing how shoddy her treatment was. Her story caused a furor, and just one year later, two emergency hospitals were built—Park Emergency Hospital on Stanyan near Golden Gate Park and Harbor Emergency Hospital at the foot of Clay near the Embarcadero. (The Park Emergency Hospital building, just north of Kezar Stadium, is still standing and is a city landmark.)

By 1903, a citywide Emergency Hospital System had been formally established. It grew to include five emergency hospitals: Park, Harbor, Central, Mission, and Alemany. Alemany was the last one built: it was funded by a bond measure that also funded the city's tuberculosis farm in San Mateo County.

The Emergency Hospital System was essentially a network of glorified first-aid stations, served by ambulances that could get to any location in the city within six minutes. Eighty percent of emergency hospital cases involved minor cuts, abrasions, lacerations, objects in eyes, insect bites, and upper-respiratory problems. But EHS staff also had to address more serious problems. Because of their locations, the five emergency hospitals each handled different types of cases. Harbor dealt with serious waterfront accidents and stevedores who were injured in brawls. Park handled dog bites, tick bites, and kids who fell off swings. Alemany, located in a working-class neighborhood, saw a lot of domestic accidents, but when they had car injuries, they were "lulus" because there were so many expressways nearby.

For residents of working-class neighborhoods such as the Excelsior, the Emergency Hospital System was a godsend. If a family's kid busted his arm or cut himself with a knife, they didn't have to go down to San Francisco General to get treatment. Many older San Franciscans fondly—well, perhaps not so fondly—remember using the various emergency hospitals.

However, the system was always financially strapped, which provided fodder for conservative critics. In 1935, the *Saturday Evening Post* ran an article attacking such New Deal experiments and singling out the "voluntary hospitals which have been operating in the red for years."

But the Emergency Hospital System carried on despite its financial woes. In 1937, it had its busiest year, with seventy thousand admissions. And praise for it poured in locally and from across the country. In 1948, the *San Francisco Chronicle* proudly noted that San Francisco was alone among U.S. cities in offering free emergency care to all its citizens. *Time* magazine called the system the most outstanding in the country.

The Emergency Hospital System remained deeply in the red, however, and in 1978, the city closed it down. Angry Excelsior residents staged a sit-in in the hospital for a month and a half. (In an ironic footnote, Supervisor Dan White—who was to assassinate Mayor George Moscone and Supervisor Harvey Milk just

months later—supported the protesters.) But it was to no avail. The system was closed for good.

The hospital and clinic buildings on Onondaga Street have been shuttered for years. But a free health clinic and an arts organization are hoping to take up occupancy in them, continuing a tradition of serving the community that started more than a century ago.

## THE LAST PIECE OF CALIFORNIO-OWNED LAND IN SAN FRANCISCO

By a weird quirk of fate, the land on or near which the Alemany Health Center stands was the last remaining parcel of the vast Californio-owned ranchos that once covered San Francisco. The final San Francisco chapter of the "California pastoral" fizzled out in a vegetable garden way out here in the sticks in 1917.

During the brief period of Mexican rule over California, Mexican authorities granted much of the land in San Francisco to a handful of Latino Californios, mostly former soldiers and civil servants, as well as one Anglo, Jacob Leese. The largest of these land grants were probably the most generous payoffs to sergeants and minor bureaucrats in history. José de Jésus Noé, for example, was the alcalde of Yerba Buena in 1842, which sounds impressive, except for the fact that Yerba Buena in 1842 had a population of about fifty people. In 1845, Noé petitioned the Mexican governor of California, Pío Pico, for a land grant, writing, "I Jose de Jesus Noé . . . present that being the owner of a number of cattle and horses; and as the same are increasing, and not having any place to keep them, I ask you Excellency . . . be pleased to grant me one square league of land . . . I have a large family, which will receive this benefit from your Excellency."

Pico granted Noé's request for Rancho San Miguel. Since a square league is about three miles by three miles, or 4,444 acres—about one-sixth of the area of present-day San Francisco—Noé presumably had ample room to keep his cattle and horses.

Today's Excelsior District was part of another vast rancho, called Rincón de las Salinas y Potrero Viejo, located south and east of Rancho San Miguel. Also a square league in size, this rancho was granted to a retired Mexican soldier at the Presidio named José Cornelio Bernal in 1839. Rincón de las Salinas means "corner of a salty marsh" and referred to the wetlands of the area's most significant stream, Islais Creek, which had two main sources—Glen Canyon and a now covered body of water near Cayuga and Geneva that was given the grandiose name Lake Geneva.

Bernal built an adobe near the site of present-day St. Luke's Hospital, on the old Mission Road that connected Mission Dolores with the other missions in the chain. After he died in 1842, his son built a house in the small Californio colony near Mission Dolores, at Seventeenth and Church.

Like the other Californios who owned much of San Francisco—and much of California, for that matter—the Bernal family ended up losing their land. The dispossession of the Californios was one of the state's founding injustices. Although the Treaty of Guadalupe Hidalgo that ended the Mexican-American War granted the Californio rancheros title to the land they had owned under Mexico, an unjust subsequent law made it so difficult for them to prove ownership that they were forced to sell their land just to pay their legal bills. Usurious compound interest rates on loans also forced many rancheros to sell.

Responsibility for the dispossession of the Californios lies overwhelmingly with the Americans. But the Californios' quasi-feudal lifestyle and famous generosity, and their unwillingness or inability to adapt to American-style capitalism, also played a role.

The latter factors seem to have contributed to the loss of the Bernal rancho—at least according to a November 8, 1926, *San Francisco Chronicle* obituary for José Cornelius Bernal, the grandson of the original grantee. The obituary noted, "The dons and their descendants lived a feudal life, giving little care to business . . . the homes of the owners were centers of hospitality. The Bernal family was no exception to the deep tradition . . . The best road from the little Mission Dolores and the Presidio to the southern missions ran at the foot of the hill where the Bernal hacienda stood. The latch string was always out, and day or night weary travelers were welcomed by the Bernal overlord. It was this carefree life and lavish generosity, coupled with the lack of good business instincts, that led to the gradual breaking up of the grants. When the owners needed money . . . they borrowed . . . They never seemed to get ahead, and little by little the vast ranchos were whittled down by foreclosure of the mortgages."

Bernal's descendants sold off the vast rancho one piece at a time, until by 1908 all that Bernal's grandson owned was one small tract—a twenty-five-acre piece used for vegetable gardens, located in a little valley on what is now Onondaga Avenue near Mission Street. When that parcel was lost to foreclosure in 1917, the days of the dons in San Francisco had come to an end, not with a bang but with a whimper.

# THE STATIONS-OF-THE-CROSS COMMUTE

San Francisco's outlying neighborhoods grew in different ways, but most had two things in common. They were initially settled by farmers or dairy farmers, and they began to urbanize only when public transportation became available—first omnibuses, then horsecars, then cable cars, and finally electric streetcars (hence the expression "streetcar suburbs").

The Mission is a good example. For the city's first three decades, it was regarded as a remote area and was populated mostly by farmers and dairy farmers, as well as housing two horse-race tracks. In the 1880s, cable cars and streetcar lines began running to the Mission and the Western Addition, which led to an explosion of new home construction; the previously outlying districts had become streetcar suburbs. As property values increased, farms were replaced with homes and businesses. An 1884 *Chronicle* article gushed that the two neighborhoods had become "two almost new cities, each as populous as the old one and the seat of the finest and most delightful residences on the peninsula."

But neighborhoods such as the Excelsior were so distant that they remained rural much longer. The Excelsior did not get its first streetcar line until 1903. Very few people who worked downtown were going to live six miles away unless there was a streetcar line nearby.

From a very early date, however, the Excelsior and the surrounding areas were served by the first train ever to run to San Francisco. In 1863, the San Francisco and San Jose Railroad opened, running from its downtown station at Fourth and Brannan to Mission Dolores, cutting through the so-called Bernal Gap between Bernal Heights and Fairmount Heights (in Glen Park), and then traversing what are now the Excelsior and Outer Mission districts on its way to the peninsula and San Jose. This was the route of El Camino Real, also known as the Old Mission Road, the venerable Spanish path that started in San Diego and ended at Mission Dolores. But although the train stopped near the Bernal adobe on the site of present-day St. Luke's, and stopped again at a station called San Miguel two miles farther west, the future Excelsior District was too sparsely populated and rural to be much affected by the train.

The first residents of the Excelsior were Irish, Italian, Swiss, and German farmers and dairy ranchers, who began arriving in the 1860s. John Consigliere, who was born in the Excelsior and whose grandfather came to San Francisco from Genoa in 1860, told the *Chronicle*, "This was quite a district. In the hills above the

Mission, it was all cows and sheep and Swiss and German people. Here you had the Italian gardeners. And the Irish worked down at City Hall." The Italian farmers grew Swiss chard, zucchini, peppers, string beans, cabbage, brussels sprouts, basil, and parsley and sold the produce downtown in the Colombo Market, the bustling wholesale produce market that opened in 1874. It was not an easy trip: it was a three-and-a-half-hour ride by horse and wagon. Since the produce needed to arrive at the stalls by three A.M. (the first buyers arrived at four A.M.), the farmers had to leave before midnight.

The Italian residents of the Excelsior faced similarly daunting logistics when they went to church. According to Consigliere, if they wanted to hear Mass given by an Italian priest, they had to travel three and a half hours to attend Mass at Saint Peter and Paul in North Beach. Alternatively, they would leave on Saturday, pick up the priest, and drive him back out to the Excelsior—an all-day excursion. The priest would spend the night with a family, say Mass the next day in a local barn, and then get a ride back to North Beach.

The devout Italians of the Excelsior, and the priests of North Beach, were finally spared this stations-of-the-cross commute in 1898, when Italians from the neighborhood built a $7,000 wooden church, Corpus Christi, about five blocks east of the Alemany Health Center.

# CHAPTER 12

# LANDS END

## CONTINENT'S END

LANDS END, THE mile-long headland between glorious Baker Beach and the venerable Cliff House, which in different incarnations has been looking over the Pacific since the Civil War, is one of the most spectacular places in any city in the world. From the Lands End trail, which runs below the top of the cliff, there are stunning vistas in three directions. To the east, the majestic Golden Gate Bridge protects the sheltered bay behind it. To the north, across the turbulent Golden Gate strait, the towering red Marin Headlands rise up, with Bolinas and—on a clear day—the white cliffs of Point Reyes visible in the distance. To the west, out of sight until the trail turns south at the extreme northeast corner of the peninsula, are the wild and enigmatic Farallon Islands, twenty-eight miles offshore. Beyond them, there's nothing but Pacific Ocean until Hawaii.

This sublime place is accompanied by a geologic and human history of equally mind-expanding scale. Take the Marin Headlands: the rock they are made of, radiolarian chert, is composed of inconceivable trillions of tiny organisms that over the aeons died and drifted down to the ocean floor until they became a mountain. North of this geologic shell mound shimmers dreamlike Point Reyes, the site of the uncanniest of all early European visits to California, Sir Francis Drake's completely random pit stop there in 1579 as he fled pursuing Spanish warships. And the Farallones ride the horizon like the legendary Manila galleon that sailed once a year down the California coast for 250 years, cruising right past the Golden Gate on its scurvy-ridden way to Acapulco. In fact, the Farallones are the reason early mariners never found the entrance to one of the world's great harbors: a Spanish navigational manual ordered them to stay outside the jagged, shark-haunted rocks.

This dramatic meeting of land and sea has drawn humans from the beginning. Indian artifacts were found near the site of the present-day visitor center. In *Men and Memories of San Francisco,* T. A. Barry and B. A. Patten recall that after horsemen had come to the end of the old Presidio Road, they "often went on over the cliff beyond the fort to Point Lobos, and to the cliff, where now the Cliff House stands," where they watched the sea lions play on Seal Rocks. Whether these riders explored the northernmost point of Lands End opposite Mile Rocks, which is the wildest and most inaccessible part of the headland, is unclear. Probably most visitors confined their explorations to the area around Point Lobos and the Cliff House, which in 1863 became easily accessible via Point Lobos Avenue, a privately built toll road.

In 1850, two enterprising businessmen erected a building atop Point Lobos, which used wooden semaphores to signal information about arriving ships to another semaphore station they had built three miles away, atop a hill then known as Loma Alta. In 1853, the first electric telegraph line was opened between the two stations, and Loma Alta became known as Telegraph Hill.

In the 1880s, Adolph Sutro, who made a fortune when he came up with a way to drain water from mines in the Comstock, acquired the Cliff House and eighty acres of land around it, which he called Sutro Heights. The philanthropic Sutro built an entertainment complex that included a new Cliff House, Sutro Baths, the world's largest indoor swimming pool, and an amusement park featuring the Firth wheel, an enormous Ferris wheel from which riders could see the Pacific.

Although Sutro's attractions drew thousands of people to the Lands End area, and the Richmond neighborhood around it was gradually built up, its sheer cliffs spared it from being developed. Now it never will be: since 1972, it has been permanently protected as part of the Golden Gate National Recreation Area.

Today the Lands End trail is well maintained and heavily used on weekends and in the summer. But as recently as the 1980s, it was underused, in disrepair, and actually dangerous. There was one notorious collapsing stretch along the cliff face where the trail was only a few feet wide. If you lost your footing, you would fall onto the slope below, and if you bounced wrong, you might go for a one-way ride onto the rocks two hundred feet below. It is a perversity of nostalgia that those of us who clambered over that death-defying trail think of those as the good old days.

## THE SUTRO BATHS

On a little pocket beach just north of the Cliff House stand San Francisco's damnedest fine ruins: the remains of Sutro Baths. When it opened in 1894, Adolph Sutro's glass palace was one of the marvels of the city, a vast swimming emporium that drew as many as eight thousand visitors a day on weekends. The baths had a long run but fell on hard times and burned down shortly after they were closed in 1966.

Thanks to some historical alchemy, these relatively new ruins look as ancient as an archaeological site in Asia Minor. Wandering around the cryptic maze of crumbling walls, as the waves crash against Fisherman's Rock, you feel as if you have stumbled upon the remains of the seaside temple of some lost civilization.

Sutro Baths started out not as a swimming complex but as a very ambitious, and very strange, tidal aquarium. After the Comstock mogul purchased the Cliff House and the land around it, he used to spend hours watching the waves crashing into the rocks at Seal Rock Beach, which was also known as Fisherman's Cove. As Robert and Mary Stewart write in *Adolph Sutro: A Biography*, "There was a place where the rock was hollowed out and Adolph liked to watch a wave fill it full, and then as the waves receded, the water would gradually spill out of its little catch basin . . . He decided he would go into partnership with the sea and build a tide pool. Although he called it an aquarium, it was to have no roof, it would be stocked solely by the animals delivered voluntarily by the sea, and it would be filled by the waves."

In 1884, Sutro began working on his living aquarium. As John A. Martini writes in *Sutro's Glass Palace,* the German immigrant built a semicircular one-hundred-by-one-hundred-foot aquarium at the north end of the beach, against the headland that marks the end of the cove. At the tip of the bluff, west of the aquarium, was a natural rock shelf that Sutro adapted into a "catch basin." This would hold water from breaking waves, which would then be passed through a subterranean tunnel into the aquarium. Sluice gates would be opened to fill the aquarium at high tide, then closed at low tide so water would drain away. Spectators, allowed in only at low tide, would view the marine life—fish, rays, sea anemones, even supposedly seals—brought into the tank by the water surging through the tunnel.

On September 3, 1887, Sutro held a public demonstration of his completed aquarium. The aquarium filled with 250,000 gallons of water, then emptied in just six minutes.

Just how well the tidal aquarium functioned is not clear, although it seems unlikely that any seals were ever carried in through the intake channels. But by now the big-dreaming Sutro was planning his future baths. He had begun sealing the mouth of the cove with a rock seawall and planned to turn most of the beach area into a swimming area that would be covered with a glass roof. Water would still come in from the catch basin, but the aquarium would be converted into a settling pool that would remove sand and seaweed from the water.

Sutro was one of San Francisco's greatest philanthropists, donating to the city, among other things, the magnificent grounds above the Cliff House, now known as Sutro Heights. However, as with most magnates before and since, his many virtues did not include modesty. His bathing complex, he proclaimed, would outdo the baths of ancient Rome: "A small place would not satisfy me. I must have it large, pretentious, in keeping with the Heights and the great ocean itself."

Fortunately for Sutro, Poseidon, who was notoriously irritated by such state-ments, appears to have missed this one—or at least delayed his revenge—and

the Sutro Baths opened for bathing in 1896. At 500 feet long and 254 feet wide, with six saltwater tanks heated to different temperatures by a boiler room and a freshwater plunge tank fed by a nearby spring, Sutro Baths was the largest indoor swimming complex in the world.

Sutro's mighty natatorium was the talk of the town, but in the end it proved to be a commercial flop. In 1910, it made a profit of only $12,000. In 1952, Sutro's family sold it to George Whitney, owner of nearby Playland at the Beach, for just $250,000. Whitney tried to upgrade it, installing a futuristic sky tram that ran from an observation deck behind the Cliff House to a new overlook above the old catch basin. But he, too, struggled to make Sutro Baths a going concern.

For five years in the postwar era, one of the most remarkable hermits in the history of San Francisco lived in two caves near Sutro Baths. In 1949, a young Chinese-American World War II veteran named Kit Hing Hui, despondent because his father had died, his mother was trapped in Communist China and he had lost touch with his younger brother, walked onto the Golden Gate Bridge, planning to jump off. "But I looked down and it was too high," he later recalled. "I was scared and lonesome. So I kept walking and finally got out by the Cliff House and Seal Rocks. I waded into the ocean but the waves scared me again and I went up the cliff."

Hui found a cave in the cliff and decided to move in. He lived there for two years, screening the entrance with branches, sleeping on a mattress he found and surviving on food he stole from nearby restaurants. He slept during the day and wandered around at night. When some boys found the cave and threw Hui's mattress into the sea, he moved into another cave, where he lived for three more years. During the more than five years he lived in the caves, Hui only spoke to another human being once. He became known as "The Phantom of Playland" after people in the area reported hearing an eerie, foreign-sounding voice singing "Skylark" and "Home on the Range." Hui later said singing those two songs helped keep him from going crazy.

Hui's solitary existence ended in 1955, when he was caught breaking into a nearby restaurant. His long-lost brother, who had made his way from China to San Francisco, read about "the cave hermit" in the paper, and the two were reunited after eighteen years. Hui became a new man overnight. Newspaper photos showed him beaming, with a new haircut and wearing a new suit of clothes. He got a job at a garment factory in Chinatown, and told reporters that he and his brother planned to open a Chinese restaurant. None of the restaurant owners wanted to press charges against him, and a judge granted him probation.

Hui's later fate cannot be established with certainty, but a veteran with his name and a birthdate that matched his age died in 2000, at the age of 78. It is pleasant to think this was indeed the former Phantom of Playland, and that he lived happily ever after.

In the 1960s, Sutro Baths was acquired by a developer who planned to erect high-rise apartments and a shopping center. Mercifully, after the flames destroyed the baths, the National Park Service acquired the 4.4-acre site in 1980. It has practiced a form of benign neglect ever since, allowing countless visitors to wander around a decaying, poetic relic.

Sutro held a typically cavalier nineteenth-century attitude toward the cove he had despoiled, saying, "The useless exemplar of geological erosion has become the home of one of humanities [sic] greatest works." But nature is having the last laugh. The wind and waves are inexorably wearing away what is left of the ruins. Eventually, there will be nothing left of them.

# THE LITTLE RAILROAD

For thirty-seven cliff-hanging years, one of the most scenic short-line railroads ever built ran through Lands End. Starting in 1888, a steam train left from Presidio and California, went out California to Thirty-Third Avenue, turned right through what is now the grounds of the Palace of the Legion of Honor, then turned left and hugged the cliff along the route of the current trail. About halfway along the route, it went through a 240-foot tunnel blasted through the cliffs near the Mile Rocks steps, then terminated at Forty-Seventh Avenue and Point Lobos, across from the entrance to Sutro Heights.

For the few minutes that it lasted, this short line offered passengers a stunning scenic ride. About half the cars were open boxcars with benches, affording passengers wide-open views of the magnificent vistas, which at the time were unblocked by trees. On the line's opening day, the press exulted that working men and women could now enjoy fresh ocean air and visit Adolph Sutro's pleasure gardens, at the reasonable cost of a nickel.

The Ferries and Cliff House Railway, the company that ran the steam train, was backed by Adolph Sutro, his cousin Gustav, and other investors. Sutro pushed for the new line not just to bring visitors to his attractions but to jab a sharp stick in the eye of the Southern Pacific, which ran a competing steam train to the Cliff House, charging a steep twenty cents for a round trip. Sutro regarded that fare as extortionate. His passion was making amenities affordable for the common man, and he despised the Octopus.

But the long-tentacled Southern Pacific was not about to give up. In 1893, it acquired the Ferries and Cliff House Railway and immediately raised the fare from five cents to a dime. In retaliation, Sutro began charging passengers on the Southern Pacific–controlled railway twenty-five cents to enter Sutro Heights, while allowing visitors who walked to enter free. When this tactic failed, Sutro opened his own electric railway line, the Sutro Railroad Company, which carried passengers to the Cliff House for a nickel.

This little railway war had consequences beyond a couple of dueling transportation franchises. Sutro's anti–Southern Pacific stance was popular with the public and helped him win election as mayor of San Francisco in 1894.

Starting in the 1890s, electric lines began replacing steam trains, and the last Lands End steam train ran in 1905. For twenty more years, electric trains kept running along the cliffs, but the slides that had plagued the line from the beginning finally proved too much to overcome. On February 7, 1925, a huge landslide below the recently opened Legion of Honor washed out hundreds of feet of track. It was the last straw: the railway never ran again.

## THE FORGOTTEN FOUNDER

Precisely because it's such an unconquerable piece of nature, Lands End has played a comparatively small role in San Francisco's history. Like Mile Rocks, the wave-swept rocks at its feet, it is impervious to the swirls and eddies of change and fate. It simply endures, facing the Marin shore across the ocean as it has done from time immemorial. So it's somehow appropriate that Lands End enters the city's history in a way that's at once mythic and obscure. It was the climax of the first European expedition to set foot in San Francisco. But that expedition, and the strange and star-crossed man who led it, is almost entirely forgotten.

The story begins on the cloudy, cold morning of December 3, 1774, when a Spanish officer named Fernando Rivera y Moncada led a party of explorers to the top of Mount Davidson, the highest point in the city. They were the first Europeans to set foot on the city's soil. Rivera and his men camped that night near Lake Merced and the next day set off to the north, looking for a clearer view of the complex system of water they had seen from the mountain.

Rivera and his men walked north on Ocean Beach, up the cliffs past the site of the future Cliff House, above Point Lobos, to the site of present-day Fort Miley. In his diary, Rivera wrote, "I succeeded in treading the beach, and came to stand upon the very point on the south side, the one with the three rocks." From this vantage point, Rivera saw and described the mouth of the Golden Gate, Mile Rocks, Angel Island, and the Marin Headlands, including Point Bonita.

The aging captain was unimpressed with barren, windy San Francisco as a site. Instead of establishing a settlement there, as his superiors wanted him to do, he headed back to Monterey. Before he left, he erected a cross on the edge of the cliff to serve as a guidepost for future parties.

Rivera was the first in a long line of Southern Californians to dismiss fog-shrouded San Francisco. But his dismissive attitude was to ruin his career and ultimately cost him his life.

At the then advanced age of forty-nine, Rivera had had a long and distin-guished career of military service to the Spanish crown. In 1752, at the age of twenty-seven, he had been appointed to command the Presidio at Loreto, in Baja

California, the northernmost outpost in New Spain. In 1769, he led the first overland party to explore present-day California, leaving six weeks before the more famous party led by Gaspar de Portolá. After helping to establish San Diego and Monterey, he bought a small farm in Guadalajara with his wife and three sons, planning to retire.

But those plans were dashed when the Spanish viceroy in Mexico, Antonio Bucareli, appointed Rivera the third military governor of California. In 1773, a reluctant Rivera recruited fifty-one settlers in Sinaloa and made the long march to Monterey. Not long after he arrived, he, like the military governor who had preceded him, had a falling-out with Junipero Serra, founder of the California missions. Serra was burning with holy zeal to establish more missions in his planned chain and was angry that Rivera was reluctant to send his troops to support them. For his part, Rivera had only sixty troops to control all of California and was afraid of spreading them too thin. Events were to prove that his fears were justified.

## RIVERA'S DOWNFALL

In 1775, Indians enraged by soldiers' rapes of native women attacked the mission at San Diego, bludgeoning a priest to death and killing two other church workers. It was the most traumatic event in the young history of the Spanish colonial enterprise.

As military governor, it was Rivera's duty to respond forcefully. He led a party to San Diego to find and punish the transgressors but was thwarted by Serra, who persuaded the Spanish viceroy to release them so that their souls could be saved. (Serra, whose holiness verged on the maniacal, did not regard the massacre as entirely a bad thing, writing, "Thanks be to God. Now that the earth has been watered by blood, the conversion of the San Diego Indians is inevitable.") When Rivera tried to seize the ringleader of the revolt, a priest excommunicated him on the spot, and Serra upheld the excommunication. The incident drove Rivera to the edge of a nervous breakdown.

Rivera's downfall started when he crossed swords with a younger, newly arrived officer, Lieutenant Colonel Juan Bautista de Anza, who had been dispatched to Monterey with vague orders to find a good spot to colonize. Rivera, who was Anza's superior, insisted that San Francisco was a worthless site, but Anza ignored him. In 1776, Anza made his famous exploration of San Francisco, choosing sites for the presidio and the mission. While he was away, Rivera appears to have become completely unhinged.

After Anza returned to Monterey, he rode a few miles south to meet Rivera. On the way, he met some soldiers who told him that Rivera had gone mad. The two men came face-to-face on their mounts. Rivera was unshaven, wrapped in blankets, with only his left eye showing under his hat. Anza greeted him and was politely inquiring about his health when Rivera abruptly said, "Goodbye, Don Juan," and spurred his mule away.

Anza regarded this bizarre breach of etiquette as a mortal insult and set out to break Rivera. Supported by his superiors, Anza held the upper hand. By the end of their poisonous feud, Rivera was reduced to pleading desperately, "For God's sake, what do you want of me?" It was no use. He was demoted to his original position as commander of the Loreto Presidio in Baja California. In a crowning (no pun intended) indignity, he was never paid.

In 1781, Rivera was ordered to lead a party of settlers from Sinaloa to Los Angeles. Along the way, he and his party were ambushed by Yuma Indians, who slaughtered them to the last man. Rivera fought bravely until he was cut down. Ironically, he ended up suffering the very fate he feared.

Today, Anza is celebrated as the founder of San Francisco, while Rivera is remembered only for lending his name to a street in the Sunset—and, by trivia buffs, for being the only person to have two city streets named after him (there is also a Moncada Way in the Ingleside). But before Rivera was sent packing in disgrace, he ordered the departure of the party of settlers that was to colonize San Francisco. As the historian Alan K. Brown notes, "With this accomplished, the captain finally, if reluctantly, had become directly responsible for the founding of San Francisco. He received little credit for it then or since."

As for the cross that Rivera erected on Lands End—the first marker placed in San Francisco—it disappeared long ago.

## THE MILE ROCKS LIGHTHOUSE

The jagged rocks off Lands End have been responsible for many of the more than 360 shipwrecks that have taken place in or just outside San Francisco Bay. The wreckage of several of those ships is visible at low tide from the Lands End trail.

One of the deadliest outcroppings is a shelf of submerged or barely visible black rocks that extends half a mile into the channel. This shelf is marked by Mile Rocks, two wave-swept rocks that face a small, stony beach a mile east of Fort Point, the Civil War–era fort at the base of the Golden Gate Bridge. The larger of the two rocks is just forty feet long and thirty feet wide. And on it was constructed one of the city's most remarkable, and lovely, structures.

The southern entrance of the Golden Gate was known to be extremely dangerous from the city's founding. A fog bell was installed at Fort Point, but ships approaching Mile Rocks often could not hear it. In 1889, engineers placed a buoy near the rocks, but in the winter the powerful ebb tides that race through the Golden Gate dragged it underwater. The engineers resignedly reported that Mile Rocks "must always be a menace to navigation as long as they exist."

It took the worst shipwreck in the city's history to galvanize officials into action. In 1901, the 370-foot passenger steamer *City of Rio de Janeiro* struck the submerged shelf off Fort Point in heavy fog. She sank in just eight minutes, taking 128 souls with her.

The Lighthouse Board, the precursor of the Coast Guard, recommended that a lighthouse be installed on Mile Rocks. The city hired a contractor named James McMahon to build it. And so began one of the most unusual and daunting construction projects in U.S. history.

McMahon sailed a schooner out to the rocks with a team of skilled builders. But when they saw their job site, a jagged black rock barely above sea level, with waves constantly washing over it, they refused to leave the ship.

Unfazed, McMahon went down to the City Front, as the Embarcadero was called, and made the rounds of sailors' haunts. He quickly recruited a team of old salts and sailed back to the rocks.

To get onto the rock, the sailors had to leap off a small boat at the top of a swell and then cling to the rock as waves washed over them. Even men used to going aloft in storms often found themselves in the water. The conditions were so harsh that the men could often work only a few hours a day. It took them a year, but they succeeded in blasting and leveling the rock and installing huge steel plates on which to build the lighthouse's massive concrete foundation.

By 1906, they had finished the job. Atop Mile Rocks rose an eighty-five-foot lighthouse shaped like a narrow, tapering wedding cake. It was equipped with a third-order Fresnel lens visible up to eighteen nautical miles away and a powerful compressed-air whistle. The deadly south side of the Golden Gate was no longer a black hole.

The Mile Rocks Lighthouse was considered one of the finest examples of a "sea-swept lighthouse"—the most dramatic of all lighthouse types—in the nation. But being posted there was not for the faint of heart. It was a "stag" lighthouse, large enough for only one keeper, so the mostly married men assigned there had to endure long separations from their families. The wife of one keeper would walk her dog on the cliffs at Lands End every night with a flashlight, which she would use to signal her husband that she was thinking of him.

Sadly, in 1965 the manned lighthouse—which is depicted in one of Lucien Labaudt's superb WPA frescoes in the Beach Chalet—was replaced with an automated light station, which also serves as an emergency helicopter landing pad. The base of the tower, constructed by sailors more than a century ago, is all that remains of what was once one of the world's most dramatic lighthouses.

# CHAPTER 13

# THE HAAS-LILIENTHAL HOUSE

## THE RECKENDORFERS

THE HAAS-LILIENTHAL HOUSE is one of the great Victorians in San Francisco, and one of the few open to the public. It also is one of the only surviving houses from an only-in-San-Francisco subculture: the Bavarian Jewish merchant princes who planted the seeds of their mighty commercial empires during the Gold Rush.

The story of the early Jewish immigrants to San Francisco is one of the most astonishing success stories in a city that has seen more than its share of them. The first remarkable thing about the men who would become pillars of the community is how many of them came from the same small region: Upper Franconia in German-speaking Bavaria. In fact, a few of them came from the same tiny town, Reckendorf, population 1,000—about the same population as Yerba Buena in 1846. William Haas, who built the Haas-Lilienthal house with money he made from his dry-goods empire, came from Reckendorf. So did Isaias Hellman, who became the state's leading banker and whose great-grandson Warren Hellman endowed one of San Francisco's most beloved annual events, the Hardly Strictly Bluegrass music festival. So did Isaac Walter, who made a fortune in home furnishings. Indeed, according to Frances Dinkelspiel, author of *Towers of Gold: How One Jewish Immigrant Named Isaias Hellman Created America*, no fewer than nine

Jewish millionaires came from this hamlet where geese and chickens ran about the unpaved streets. The most famous Jewish merchant of them all, Levi Strauss, grew up in a town just twenty miles away.

In Bavaria—which was an independent state until Germany became a unified country in 1871—Jews faced bigotry and restrictive laws. There had been bloody anti-Semitic riots in the nearby town of Wurzburg as recently as 1819, and Jews were still regarded by much of the majority-Catholic population as outsiders and economic threats. They were not allowed to work as brewers or in other elite professions, and an infamous list called the Matrikel prevented a Jew from moving into a town until another Jew died, making it almost impossible for young men to marry and start families. As a result of these restrictions, starting in 1840, large numbers of German Jews began immigrating to the United States. Between 1840 and 1870, more than 20,000 of Bavaria's 59,000 Jews immigrated, joining thousands from Prussia and France. Between 1850 and 1860, the number of Jews in the United States tripled, from 50,000 to 150,000. By 1880, it had gone up to 280,000.

Many came to San Francisco. By the mid-1870s, 16,000 Jews were living there, and by the 1880s, it had a larger Jewish population than any city in the country except New York.

Most of these Bavarian Jewish immigrants arrived with only a few dollars. But they had other assets: good educations, experience in trade in the old country, and in many cases family connections in their new country. Armed with these, ambition, and a strong work ethic, and finding themselves in a wide-open frontier town unhindered by anti-Semitism, they succeeded beyond their wildest dreams.

## THE GROCER MAKES GOOD

The story of the man who built the Haas-Lilienthal house, William Haas, is typical of the Bavarian Jews who made a fortune in San Francisco. Haas was a member of one of the leading Jewish families in Reckendorf, which dealt in cotton and textiles. Barely twenty when he arrived in San Francisco in 1868, he went to work in a wholesale grocery company started by his brother Kalman, who had arrived in 1851. Like many Jews during the Gold Rush, Kalman had realized that "mining the miners" was a much better way to get rich than mining for gold.

Haas started as a clerk, sometimes sleeping on a shelf in the store, then worked his way up to salesman, then partner. The California Street business dealt in coffee, tea, canned goods, and cigars and traded with Japan, China, Mexico, and

Australia. Within two years, Haas bought a modest $1,000 house. By 1886, he had become a wealthy man and could afford the princely sum of $18,000, not including the land and furnishings, to build a magnificent three-story Queen Anne Victorian at 2007 Franklin Street.

Haas and his wife, Bertha, had three children. According to Irena Narell in *Our City: The Jews of San Francisco*, Haas was a benevolent patriarch who "ruled the roost with great authority, tempering autocratic decisions with kindness and generosity. Preoccupied with business as a way of life, he still managed to make his wife Bertha and the children his central concern. William read German authors; studied English with the aid of a dictionary; and read Keats, Shelley, Chaucer, Burns and Byron. Oliver Wendell Holmes' 'The Autocrat at the Breakfast Table' was a favorite and occupied a prominent place on his study shelves. For relaxation there was fishing, tennis, photography, and operattas at the Tivoli Theater."

Haas's boyhood friends from Reckendorf had enjoyed the same tremendous success and had taken up residence in the same exclusive part of the city. Isaias Hellman lived just two blocks away at Franklin and Sacramento, and Isaac Walter's house was even closer. The three men, part of what they half-jokingly called the Reckendorf aristocracy, usually walked to work downtown together.

All three Reckendorfers returned regularly to their birthplace to visit friends and family. As Dinkelspiel writes, "Even though they had fled in their youth from towns that restricted opportunities for Jews, they spoke to their children in German [and] regarded the culture as superior to that in America." In 1911, William and Bertha Haas, wandering nostalgically around Reckendorf's still unpaved streets, were surprised to run into Isaac Walter and Isaias Hellman. They passed a pleasant afternoon in their hometown, perhaps marveling at the hand that fate had dealt them.

## A UNIQUE JEWISH ELITE

San Francisco's German Jewish elite was unique in the United States. No other Jewish community succeeded in business so rapidly, was so acculturated, uninterested in religion, and accepted by gentile society.

There were a number of reasons for the cosmopolitan nature of San Francisco's Jewish aristocracy. First, Jews in San Francisco encountered far less anti-Semitism than they did on the East Coast. The instant city that sprang up during the Gold Rush was too anarchic, self-invented, and filled with people of all sorts from all over the world to be ruled by social pecking orders. "All nations having come hither, shades of color, of belief, peculiarities of physique, of temper and habit were less distinctly marked," observed the historian Hubert Bancroft. And East Coast notions of class hierarchy had no sway in a place where former judges worked as common laborers and former ditch diggers rode down the street in fancy carriages.

Anti-Semitism in San Francisco was also undercut by the fact that one of its traditional tropes, the idea that Jews were greedy money hogs, was the motivating force behind the entire Gold Rush. It would have been the height of hypocrisy for any forty-niner to attack Jews for wanting to get rich. As Bancroft wrote, "Gold was here, and in common with the Gentiles Jews loved gold . . . Money was the humanizing bond . . . Christian and Jew loved money."

Nor did anti-Semitism grow as the city matured. The 1879 *Elite Directory* included many Jews, something unthinkable in any other city in the country at the time.

Contributing to the gentile acceptance of the Jewish community was the fact that the latter was neither insular nor separatist (except when it came to marriage) nor particularly religious. The young, mostly male, ambitious, and risk-taking Jews who came to San Francisco were not very devout to begin with, and as they

became more and more wealthy and successful, their attachment to Judaism grew weaker still. As the historian Fred Rosenbaum notes in *Visions of Reform: Congregation Emanu-El and the Jews of San Francisco 1849–1999*, at the end of the 1870s only 16 percent of sixteen thousand Jews belonged to one of the city's seven synagogues.

A well-known rabbi who visited the city in the 1870s commented, "'I take no interest in Jewish affairs' is a remark you hear 10 times a day by men of prominence." Irena Narell writes, "For the majority of socially prominent San Francisco Jews, religious affiliation was primarily a matter of form." She quotes one of William Haas's descendants as saying, "My mother was an atheist but paid Temple dues so she could be buried in the Jewish cemetery. My father did not set foot in a temple. My grandmother (a Sloss) *never* went, even on High Holy Days. But she wouldn't leave the house on a Jewish holiday, nor be seen downtown or in a restaurant, because what would the gentiles think of such lack of respect!"

The fact that San Francisco's Jews encountered so little anti-Semitism also contributed to their feeble attachment to religion—and led many to oppose Zionism. Julius Kahn, who represented San Francisco in Congress for more than twenty years—and, like banker Isaias Hellman and other prominent San Francisco Jews, was strongly opposed to the proposal to create a Jewish state in British-controlled Palestine—said, "The United States is my Zion and San Francisco is my Jerusalem."

## AN INBRED ARISTOCRACY—
## AND AN ENDURING LEGACY

San Francisco's Jewish aristocracy was acculturated and not religious, but it was not completely assimilated. Very few members of the two or three dozen families that made up the Jewish elite married non-Jews. And since it was unthinkable that a member of that aristocracy would marry someone of a lower class, this meant that the prospective marriage pool was extremely small: it was made up almost entirely of the Slosses, Lilienthals, Hellmans, Gerstles, Koshlands, Walters, Dinkelspiels, and a few other families. Most of these clans lived in mansions in one patrician area, on Van Ness, Franklin, or Gough between Post and Pacific. "By World War I, the city's Jewish aristocracy had become so inbred it almost resembled the royalty of Europe," Rosenbaum wrote. In one example of such aristocratic marriages, William Haas's daughter Alice married Sam Lilienthal, who was himself the product of a marriage between two wealthy Jewish families, the Lilienthals and the Slosses.

The social hierarchies observed by San Francisco's Jewish aristocracy were as rigid as the most ossified distinctions enforced by snobbish East Coast WASP elites. Only Jews from Bavaria, Hesse, or Bohemia, or French Jews from Alsace, were admitted to the elite. Polish Jews were seen as déclassé. As Harriet Lane Levy, a Polish Jew, wrote in *920 O'Farrell Street: A Jewish Girlhood in Old San Francisco*, "That the Baiern [Bavarians] were superior to us, we knew . . . On the social counter the price tag 'Polack' confessed second class. Why Poles lacked the virtues of Bavarians I did not understand, though I observed that to others the inferiority was as obvious as it was to us that our ash man and butcher were of poorer grade than we, because they were ash man and butcher . . . Upon this basis of discrimination everybody agreed and acted."

When large numbers of impoverished, Yiddish-speaking Eastern European and Russian Jews began pouring into the United States in the 1890s, San Francisco's German Jewish elite reacted with alarm. The city's leading rabbi, Jacob Voorsanger of the elite synagogue Temple Emanu-El, warned that the new immigrants' proclivity to "herd together and refuse to scatter" would lead gentiles to lump together the integrated German Jewish "Israelites" with "Yiddish mumblers." But the elites nonetheless offered financial and social work assistance to the newcomers, most of whom lived South of Market and in the Fillmore, and over time the gulf between the two groups narrowed.

And the Jewish elite's benevolence extended beyond their coreligionists. From the nineteenth century until today, San Francisco's Jewish community has been noteworthy for its civic-mindedness. In a very real sense, Jews built San Francisco. Jewish philanthropists have created and supported a remarkable number of institutions and amenities across the city, from hospitals, universities, and charities to museums, promenades, parks, pools, and much more.

Some of those gifts were personal. In 1972, the descendants of the Haas and Lilienthal families donated the family mansion on Franklin, one of the great surviving Victorians in San Francisco, to San Francisco Heritage, ensuring that a majestic piece of the city's history would not only survive but be open to all.

For a handful of immigrants from small towns in Bavaria who arrived in California with little but their wits, these gifts to the city that welcomed them are an enduring legacy.

## THE VICTORIAN STYLE

Ask any San Francisco resident or visitor to come up with a list of the ten most characteristic things about the city, and "Victorians" is certain to be on it. Those ornate redwood confections, which in their later phases were filled with enough curving bay windows, sandcastle turrets, gratuitous spires, and ornamental wood-work to keep a factory of lathes spinning for Queen Victoria's entire sixty-three-year reign, are as inseparably associated with the city of St. Francis as the cable cars, the Golden Gate Bridge, the bay, the fog, and the hills. In a city where too many new buildings are cheap modernist knockoffs that have all the charm of a giant plastic Legoland crossed with an Olympic Village circa 1964 Bucharest, they offer an escape into another age. They offer the appeal of the antique.

And yet these antiques are delightfully paradoxical. For one thing, they are exuberant and overblown—show-offy, rococo, in your face. These are not qualities we associate with "Victorian," a word that usually evokes the stodgier qualities of solidity, conservatism, patriarchy, prudence. But that association—indeed, that entire way of seeing the late nineteenth century—is as simplistic as dismissing the 1950s as an age of conservatism. For the Victorian period was a dynamic and hopeful time, marked by a great expansion of homeownership, and its architecture reflects that expansive optimism. Victorian houses represented a brave new middle-class world, a growing democracy of domesticity that was self-assured enough to flower into a boastful and flamboyant architecture. For its proud owners, that flashy new Queen Anne house was the 1880s equivalent, mutatis mutandis, of a Tesla or a rap song. Check out my big-ass turret, homies!

The second paradox of the city's Victorians is hidden, but perhaps even more important. As Randolph Delehanty and Richard Sexton write in *In the Victorian Style*, "The San Francisco Victorian house was essentially *modern*. The key to understanding it lies not in its obvious façade but in its invisible plumbing. It was born out of a fascination with two things: new technologies and the architectural styles of the past. In how it was built, sold, financed, and served (by streetcars, municipal sewers, running water, gas, electricity, and even telephones), the San Francisco Victorian row house was radically new, not old-fashioned . . . It is the tension between looking old and being new that makes Victorian houses so interesting."

Today, with San Francisco real estate values the highest in the country, even the most modest of the city's large stock of Victorian homes (a 1975–1976 survey of nine neighborhoods found 13,487 of them) are generally worth well over $1 million each—and the more opulent ones far more than that. But when they were built, most were aimed at working- and middle-class buyers, and many were priced very reasonably. As the historian Theodore Hittell wrote in 1878, San Francisco had more millionaires than other American cities, but "at the same time fewer paupers, more landowners, and more comfort in the homes of the multitude."

The "multitude" were able to buy those comfortable Victorian homes thanks to two innovative financing institutions: homestead associations and savings and loans. Homestead associations were joint stock companies that used members' fees to buy up tracts of land, which members then purchased from the association. The members hired their own contractors to build their houses. At their peak, there were more than 170 homestead associations, and they were responsible for the development of large areas of San Francisco. Savings and loans provided low-interest home loans, often to working-class Irish and other ethnic groups.

What made it possible for contractors to turn out thousands of affordable houses was a new building technology known as balloon framing. Developed in Chicago in the 1830s, balloon framing—also known as stick construction—replaced the old pegged and mortised houses, which required highly skilled carpenters. Along with mass-produced nails, uniform lumber sizes, and new tools such as lathes and routers, balloon framing allowed unskilled carpenters to build houses quickly.

These advances in construction techniques, together with a ready supply of easily worked redwood (much of it shipped from the Pacific Northwest on coastwise lumber lines like the Nelson Steamship Company), were responsible for an explosion of housing construction. As Judith Lynch Waldhorn and Sally Woodbridge note in *Victoria's Legacy*, during the 1880s and 1890s, the two major decades of house construction, "more than 1500 individuals were building, moving and remodeling houses in San Francisco." This number included more than seven hundred contractors, about four hundred architects, and several hundred owner-builders. The most productive of those contractor-builders, Fernando Nelson, built more than four thousand houses, selling many for as little as $750.

The Haas-Lilienthal house, representing the wealthiest end of the Victorian spectrum, embodies all the virtues of its genre: it is elegant, joyous, and buoyant. But the same holds true for the more modest Victorians that are found throughout so much of San Francisco. Whether austere Italianate, highly decorated stick, or asymmetrical, soaring Queen Anne, they all reflect the forward-looking modernism of a young, vigorous city. Even when they are ungainly and ostentatious, there is something lighthearted about their excess that redeems them. As Thomas Aidala writes in *The Great Houses of San Francisco*, "In the frenzy of an explosively growing nation, a city was put together out of buildings that roar with fun, that never (or almost never) take themselves so seriously as to forget to smile—and they smile well." The Fresno-born Armenian-American writer William Saroyan, whose most famous work is *The Time of Your Life*, a play set in a famous Pacific Avenue saloon called Izzy Gomez's, noted the same thing: "Any building is liable to break out into a big smile at any moment and suddenly seem no longer ugly but beautiful."

In a famous piece written after the 1906 earthquake titled "The City That Was," writer Will Irwin called San Francisco "the gayest, lightest hearted, most pleasure loving city of the western continent." The city was mostly destroyed by the catastrophe. But its spirit was uncrushed. And the Victorian houses that survived are reminders—smiling ones—of that spirit.

# CHAPTER 14

# SHIPLEY STREET

## THE SWAMPS OF MISSION BAY

By its very nature, the catastrophe that shook and burned San Francisco for three terrible days starting on April 18, 1906, left few reminders. Some buildings damaged by the earthquake might have become battle-scarred monuments if they had survived, but almost all were consumed by the flames. There are a few buildings in Chinatown and in the Jackson Square area built with "clinker" bricks blackened by the fire, but they are the exception. The disaster left the city a virtual tabula rasa.

But there is one notable exception: the South of Market area. The streets and alleys around Howard and Folsom and Sixth and Seventh bear silent witness to the single geologic phenomenon that made the quake so destructive and deadly: landfill. "Made land," as it was called at the time, was responsible for most of the deaths caused by the earthquake itself and many of those caused by the ensuing fires. And nowhere was the physical devastation, and the toll in human lives, higher than in the densely populated area between Fifth and Eighth and Mission and Bryant, on the main throughways and on alleys and side streets including Minna, Clementina, Clara, Natoma, Russ, Moss, Tehama, and the short street depicted here, Shipley.

It all started with Mission Bay and the wetlands that once surrounded its shoreline. Today, Mission Bay has been reduced to a four-block-long stretch of Mission Creek, which runs just south of the Giants' stadium before disappearing into a huge culvert near Seventh Street. But when the forty-niners arrived, Mission Bay was a 260-acre tidal cove, surrounded by saltwater marshes and fed by Mission Creek, a sinuous freshwater stream that extended along the site of present-day Division Street all the way to Mission Dolores.

These wetlands were what drew the native people, the Yelamu (also known as the Ramaytush), to the barren, sandy, windswept San Francisco peninsula in the first place. The squishy marshes were a food paradise, teeming with birds, fish, shellfish, and edible plants. The Yelamu established a winter village, Sitlintac, on the shores of Mission Bay near present-day Oracle Park.

Mission Bay enters written history on August 2, 1775, after the Spanish packet *San Carlos* sailed through the Golden Gate, the first ship to do so. Pilot Juan Bautista Aguirre was dispatched to explore the bay in a redwood dugout called a cayuco. As he sailed into Mission Bay, he observed three Indians weeping on the shore. To commemorate this sighting, he named the tidal cove Ensenada de los Llorones—Cove of the Weepers. No one will ever know why those three Indians were weeping. But the image is painfully apt, as if those nameless Indians had a foreshadowing of the terrible fate that was about to befall their people. It would not be the last time tears were shed on the edge of Mission Bay.

## THE SINKING MISSION PLANK ROAD

For the forty-niners, the Mission Bay swamps were a barrier to settlement. Those who moved into the South of Market area put up their tents or crude structures on the northern edges of the wetlands, in Happy Valley around what is now Mission and New Montgomery streets, or near Rincon Hill on the southern end of Yerba Buena Cove. Only a few hardy pioneers erected any buildings closer to the marshes.

One who did was a German immigrant named Christian Russ, who in 1851 opened San Francisco's first "pleasure garden," Russ's Gardens, on the Mission Plank Road. Russ's Gardens was especially popular with the city's large German population. In 1863, Russ moved his resort into the heart of the swamp, on the southwest corner of Sixth and Harrison, on the edge of Mission Bay. Russ's Gardens was accessible only by a road so narrow that if a rider fell off his horse, he would land in the swamp—a fact that does not seem to have deterred visitors from consuming large quantities of strong, German-brewed beer. (A nearby alley commemorates Russ.) "As late as '55, we have seen horses and cows swamped on

both sides of the Folsom street plank-road, and on the east side of the road leading to the garden," Barry and Patten write in *Men and Memories of San Francisco in the "Spring of '50."* Just how deep the Mission Bay marshes were was demonstrated in 1851, when workmen were installing the Mission Plank Road, which ran on the site of today's Mission Street between downtown and Mission Dolores. When the workers got to Seventh Street, they ran into a swamp about a hundred yards long. They had planned to erect a bridge across it, but the pilings they tried to drive as supports sank eighty feet into the marsh, forcing them to abandon the pilings and use log platforms instead. The resulting bridge shook every time a heavy team drove across it and gradually settled until it was about five feet lower than it had originally been.

In 1878, the historian J. S. Hittell noted that in the South of Market area there were three hundred acres of made land, reclaimed from two large swamps. "These were called swamps; but they seem to have been for part of their area at least, subterranean lakes, from 40 to 80 feet deep, covered by a crust of peat eight or ten feet deep," he wrote. Hittell recounted that a cow searching for grass jumped onto what appeared to be solid ground and vanished without a trace into the muck. "Many ludicrous scenes occurred in filling up the swamps . . . More than once a contractor had put on enough sand to raise the street to the official grade, and gave notice to the city engineer to inspect the work, but in the lapse of a day between the notice and inspection, the sand had sunk down six or eight feet." As a result of this subsidence, the lighter peat was crowded up eight or ten feet above street surface by the heavy sand and also pushed sideways, "so that houses and fences built upon it were carried away from their original position and tilted up at singular angles by the upheaval."

Hittell's account of what happened to the houses built on the swamplands would be an exact description of what happened to much larger buildings, packed with hundreds of people, just twenty-eight years later.

## THE COLLAPSE

In 1906, South of Market was the second most densely populated area in San Francisco (Chinatown was first), a warren of narrow, crowded streets filled with cheap rooming houses and hotels, saloons and corner stores, barbershops and small businesses. And within South of Market, one of the most highly concentrated areas was Sixth Street between Mission and Howard. On the west side of this block stood four large boardinghouses: the Brunswick House, the Ohio, the Lormor, and the Nevada. A block away, at Sixth and Folsom, stood a three-story

hotel called the Corona House. All were wood-framed buildings erected on standard foundations.

At 5:12 A.M. on April 18, 1906, a section of the Pacific Plate, the largest tectonic plate on earth, broke free from the North American Plate under the ocean floor six miles northwest of Mussel Rock, Daly City. The unimaginable energy released by this geologic shift caused shock waves to race east at seven thousand miles an hour, furrowing the ground as they went. Four seconds later they crashed into San Francisco.

The shock waves hit the reclaimed wetlands South of Market harder than any other part of the city. According to the official 1908 report on the earthquake, coauthored and edited by Andrew Lawson, professor of geology at UC Berkeley, "Only in very close proximity to the fault was greater violence manifested. For blocks the land surface, paved streets and building plots alike, were thrown into wave forms . . . street lines were shifted eastward out of their former straight courses by amounts varying from three to six feet . . . The shaking caused the materials used in filling to settle together and occupy less space, so that the surface over the whole district was lowered by amounts varying from a few inches to 3 feet or more."

The shock waves shook the marshy land South of Market so violently that the soil liquefied. The five boardinghouses on Sixth Street, and dozens of other buildings built on what Lawson called "this old swampy district," dropped into the mire, their foundations and beams cracking under the enormous strain. Like a row of dominoes, the four rooming houses between Natoma and Howard knocked each other down—the Nevada falling onto the Lormor, the Lormor falling onto the Ohio, the Ohio falling onto the Brunswick, and the Brunswick falling over on Howard Street. A block away, the Corona House sank two stories into the marsh, its ceilings and floors collapsing upon the dozens of people inside.

Some of the people living on the top floors managed to climb out of the wreckage. But many of the more than one thousand men, women, and children living in those five buildings, most of them working-class, many of them immigrants, were crushed. A doctor who rushed to the Brunswick reported hearing "a terrible, low, heart-rending cry of utter resignation" from those in the building. And those who were killed immediately were the lucky ones. Almost all of those who were trapped in the wreckage burned to death.

Just a few feet away from the Brunswick House stood a firehouse, Company Number Six. When the earthquake hit, the back wall of the firehouse sank more than three feet into the earth and the floor split down the middle. The doors of the engine house were hurled open and the company's terrified horses ran away. Captain Charles Cullen and his six-man engine crew managed to haul their heavy machine out of the wrecked firehouse, only to find out that none of the hydrants on the block had water. In fact, almost no hydrants in the city had water: the earthquake had broken the water mains. (Miraculously, a single hydrant at the top of Dolores Park was found to be working. Using its water, an army of San Franciscans—firemen, policemen, and 3,000 citizens—saved the Mission District south of 20th Street. The still-existing Greenberg hydrant is painted gold every April 18.)

Most of the buildings on the street had collapsed. Cries for help were coming from all sides. Cullen and his men rushed to the building next door and managed to rescue five adults and three children. Then they ran to the Corona House at the end of the block and began feverishly chopping with their axes at the roof, which had dropped down two stories. Screams were coming from deep inside the wreckage. "At this time my crew helped rescue a man and a woman from the Corona House," Cullen told an insurance commission later, but "approximately 40 people were killed by the collapsing of this hotel. The two survivors rescued were pinned on the top floor near a sky-light."

Such tragedies were taking place all across the former Mission Bay swamp and in other parts of town where buildings had been erected on old waterways.

## THE WETLANDS STRIKE BACK—AGAIN

Superficially, it appeared that San Franciscans had conquered the despised wetlands that stood in the way of growth and progress. They had raced to fill them with sand and debris and sold them as lots and built houses and streets on them. But the wetlands had only been biding their time. Like the return of the repressed, they had suddenly reappeared in 1906.

Eighty-three years later, they would do so again. And this time I saw the results with my own eyes.

At 5:12 P.M. on October 17, 1989, a 6.9-magnitude earthquake that originated near Loma Prieta Peak in the Santa Cruz Mountains hit San Francisco. I was living in an apartment at Jackson and Jones, on the graywacke bedrock of Nob Hill, and the only damage to my place was that a brick-and-board bookcase fell over. Within a few minutes, I had jumped on my bike and set off on a wild ride across town, chasing the quake. The first place I headed was to Gino and Carlo in North Beach. No one knew what was going on except that the earth had sucker punched our city. The bartenders were pouring free drinks. When I walked out onto Green Street, I saw a giant plume of smoke coming from the west. I jumped on my bike and sped over toward the Marina District. When I got there it was on fire. Everything was chaos and flames and shouting firemen and no one stopped me from riding right up to a building on the corner of Cervantes and Fillmore. It had been built on the edge of an old marsh—part of the same watery maze of bogs and sinuous streams out of which Maybeck had dug the lagoon for the Palace of Fine Arts—and it had collapsed. The ground floor was splintered, squished, compressed in places to two feet high. Two adults, a man and a forty-year-old woman, and a three-month-old baby had died in there an hour earlier.

At eleven thirty P.M. I rode down a South of Market alley called Bluxome, in the heart of the old Mission Bay swamp. A brick building on the east side of the street had collapsed, killing five people. Crushed cars had been pulled out into the middle of the alley. A man had been decapitated in one. An ordinary street I had gone past a thousand times had turned into a scene of horror.

Four decades after the Mission Bay wetlands had announced their presence, the unimaginable power of water—not in a dramatic tsunami or a raging flood or a mighty waterfall, but in prosaic mud—had taken another terrible toll on San Francisco.

## THE BURIED HOUSES OF SHIPLEY STREET

All of the wooden buildings built South of Market on the former wetlands were damaged in the quake. Many, like the Corona House, sank into the mud; some lost walls; others fell over sideways. No one will ever know for sure, because almost none of these buildings survived the great fires that ravaged the city for three days after the earthquake. (A rare exception was Dore Street, near Bryant and Eighth: Lawson's official report includes remarkable photographs of the havoc wreaked there.) But even though the buildings are long gone, the neighborhood's side streets bear eloquent testimony to the subsidence of unstable terrain that was responsible for so much death and destruction.

One of the most dramatic examples of subsidence is found at 274 Shipley. The former garages of this red apartment house are now five or six feet below street level: only the tops of the garage doors are above the ground. The effect is surreal, as if the house were a toy building half-buried in a sandbox—which is actually pretty much what it is. A resident in one of the apartments told me his hallway is considerably out of level.

This house, and the roughly two dozen other buried houses on Clementina, Clara, Tehama, Natoma, Moss, Russ, and other side streets, ended up as semicaves because of subsidence and subsequent grading. After the 1906 quake the marshy land in the area continued to subside, causing streets and houses to sink as much as five or six feet. In 1930 and again in 1950, the city raised the streets and utilities to grade, but it was too expensive to raise all the buildings, so many ended up half-buried.

The second evidence of subsidence is the side streets themselves. The main streets, such as Howard and Sixth and Folsom, were periodically raised to official grade, but the side streets were not raised as often. As a result, a number of them are significantly lower than the main streets. Moss and Natoma streets are so depressed they almost feel as though they're lowlands in the Sacramento River delta, with the main streets the dikes.

There used to be more half-buried houses scattered around this area, but the 1989 quake damaged a number of them and they were torn down. Like old prizefighters, the survivors are battered and bowed but still standing.

But the most poetic reminder of the wetlands that once covered much of this neighborhood is gone. A lot at 281 Clara was fenced off and left vacant for so many years that it returned to its original marshy state: a photograph taken in 1976 shows the small patch of ground completely covered in high marsh grass. Fifteen or twenty years ago, the lot was developed. With it, the last remnant of the Mission Bay wetlands—those 260 acres of mucky soil that attracted wild birds and Indians, thwarted settlers, and caused innumerable tragedies on a spring day 113 years ago—disappeared from view. But they're not gone.

# CHAPTER 15

# INA COOLBRITH PARK

## THE LADDER AT THE EDGE OF THE BLUFF

ONE OF THE most spectacular views in San Francisco is offered by little Ina Coolbrith Park on Vallejo and Taylor, a half block below the highest of Russian Hill's three summits. More a winding walkway than a conventional park, this relatively little-known space overlooks downtown San Francisco, Telegraph Hill, the Bay Bridge, and a piece of the north bay. Because the park is so close to downtown, the view has an almost hallucinatory immediacy. Yet the park also feels strangely isolated, as if it were atop a sheer alpine peak with a wide river and a forest between it and the gleaming towers.

The summit of Russian Hill has always felt like this. And in the nineteenth and early twentieth centuries, it really was cut off from the city below. The only way up to the top of the hill was a narrow foot trail, used by goats as well as people. As the Russian Hill historian William Kostura writes, "For many years only the hardier and more sure-footed pedestrians ascended the zig-zag route which had been cut into Vallejo Street's sandstone cliff; most others detoured two blocks south to Pacific." After grading in the 1860s and 1870s left a sheer bluff on Jones Street, access from the west side of the hill became even more difficult: to get to the summit of Vallejo from Jones Street, you had to climb a rickety ladder leaning against the bluff.

Its inaccessibility, combined with the fact that it was so close to downtown and North Beach, led many residents and observers to comment that Russian Hill felt like a place apart, an ethereal domain floating above the city. Prominent hill resident George Livermore wrote, "We lived virtually 'downtown' in a world city, but remained insulated by the quiet of the three streets that dead-ended into our quiet world." In an 1896 short story, Emma Frances Dawson wrote, "I live in a region of remote sounds. On Russian Hill I look down as from a balloon . . ." A now forgotten artist named Giuseppe Cadenasso lived in an artists' colony in a studio described by an early-twentieth-century observer as "perched in air like a bird cage."

These heights provided an Olympian platform from which Russian Hill denizens could observe the raucous city below. An 1860s newspaperman named O. P. Fitzgerald described looking down at the young toughs of North Beach, roistering in the valley a few hundred yards away. "The North Beach rabble in its ordinary mood is rather noisy and demonstrative," Fitzgerald wrote. "The hoodlum reaches his perfection here. The hoodlum is a young Californian in the intermediate state between a wharf rat and a desperado, combining all the sad qualities of both."

Some of those "noisy and demonstrative" youth also lived atop Russian Hill, where they made life difficult for a certain famous aesthete. "One summit resident who often chose to descend the zig-zag trail to Taylor Street was the writer and editor Gelett Burgess, who lived at the corner of Vallejo and Florence in the 1890s," Kostura writes. "He was short of stature and liked to affect a dandified appearance, so he was a natural target for the tough Italian boys who lived at Vallejo and Jones. Burgess avoided them by heading east instead of west."

## RUSSIAN HILL'S GRIM ENTRANCE INTO HISTORY

No one knows for sure who first set foot on Russian Hill. But surely at some point the first San Franciscans, the Yelamu, wandered up the narrow north–south ridge to drink from the springs that were plentiful at the top of what is now the crooked street as recently as the early twentieth century. No native artifacts have been found on the hill, although in the nineteenth century the remains of an Indian were unearthed at its base, near the Buena Vista café.

The first Spanish explorers in San Francisco may also have set foot on Russian Hill. When Captain Juan Bautista de Anza arrived on his famous expedition in June 1776, he might have ridden up to the hill's summit: a cryptic dotted line on

a map drawn by the expedition's cartographer, diarist, and resident moralistic blowhard, Father Pedro Font, indicates that after selecting the site for the presidio, Anza and his party rode south toward what is now the Mission District, where they founded Mission Dolores. The flattest route would have been down the Van Ness corridor. If they went that way, it seems likely that Anza would have ridden a quarter mile out of his way to the east to see what was on the other side of that hill.

Putting such conjectures aside, Russian Hill enters history for the first time on a decidedly grim note. On December 10, 1852, a Mexican named Jose Forni was hanged near the top of the hill—the first person to be legally executed in the young city. Forni had been convicted of murdering a man named Rodriguez in Happy Valley, near the present-day Palace Hotel, and sentenced to death. The authorities originally proposed that he be hanged in front of the county jail on Broadway (where the Beat Museum now stands), but they then decided to hang him atop Russian Hill, around what is now the minipark on Vallejo between Taylor and Jones, so that the entire town could stare up at the awful wages of crime. However, this Michel Foucault–like spectacle proved to be too much for official stomachs, and the gallows was moved one hundred yards to the west, closer to Jones Street. This less visible site still attracted an enormous crowd: ten thousand spectators climbed the hill to watch Forni drop to his death.

## HOW RUSSIAN HILL GOT ITS NAME

Just how Russian Hill got its name is unknown. The most widespread theory, however, is that it was named for unknown Russian sailors who were buried on the corner of Vallejo and Jones—the same location where a ladder leaning against a bluff once provided the only way to the summit. In 1850, the journalist Bayard Taylor reported seeing several graves with Cyrillic writing and black Orthodox crosses at that site. In 1915, several skeletons were unearthed there when Willis Polk installed his beaux arts balustrade and ramp.

Russian ships regularly entered San Francisco Bay before the Gold Rush, including one bearing a young nobleman, Nikolai Rezanov, whose star-crossed 1806 romance with the governor's daughter, a young woman named Concepcion "Conchita" Arguello, is perhaps the saddest love story in the city's history. Rezanov sailed home to ask the czar for permission to marry Conchita, but while riding across Siberia on the way back to California, he fell from his horse, fell sick, and died. According to tradition, Conchita never learned of his fate and waited for most of her life for him to return, spurning all other men. Late in life she took holy vows and spent her remaining years in a Dominican convent.

A less lofty tale involving a Russian could also be responsible for the hill's name.

The historian Rand Richards speculates that Russian Hill could have taken its name from a notorious incident that took place in 1847 in Alfred Ellis's bar near Clark's Point. After midnight one November evening, a Sausalito ship's carpenter and bar regular named George fell into the twenty-three-foot-deep well next to the bar. When he was fished out, he mumbled something about how the man he had fallen on top of had made a terrible noise. But since George was usually two sheets to the wind, no one paid any attention: they gave him a couple of drinks and sent him on his way. Over the next four days, however, the well water became first undrinkable, then so foul it could not be used even for washing. When bar owner Ellis had the well cleaned, workers found a man's hair floating on the surface, and then found the rotting body of a Russian sailor who had fallen into the well and drowned, presumably after George had fallen on him.

This discovery horrified the town, since most of its inhabitants had been to Ellis's saloon during the past four days and had drunk the contaminated water. Several leading citizens became violently ill. Richards speculates that the sailor's body was removed and buried on a nearby hill, which was forever after immortalized as "the Russian's hill."

Whether this theory is true or not, the most noteworthy thing about the dead-Russian-in-the-well incident may be that most of the citizens of Yerba Buena had been in Ellis's saloon over a four-day stretch—a manifestation of community solidarity that contemporary San Franciscans, in the time of coronavirus, have matched, and even exceeded, in reverse. As this book goes to press, none of us have been in any saloons for seven weeks—a feat of civic-mindedness that the forty-niners could only dream of.

## THE BOHEMIAN YEARS

From the city's early days, Russian Hill's isolation, beauty, and affordability attracted writers, artists, and poets. In a 1912 article in the *San Francisco Call* titled "Russian—the Hill of Those Who Love It," Mabel H. Collyer wrote that before the millionaires arrived, "the hill became a sort of poets' corner. Only the true art lovers, it seems, were willing to scale the heights. The artists followed the poets and the writers followed the artists, and these disciples of the muses, making their own bit of Bohemia, gave the hill a prestige that was not without a hint of exclusiveness. And this has lasted even to the present day. As early as the '60s the weeds in the goat path had been trampled flat by art devotees."

Poet, writer, and librarian Ina Coolbrith—California's first poet laureate—who lived in various homes on Russian Hill for most of her life, wrote, "We were all hillites. There were no streetcars, only clumsy, lumbering omnibuses which jolted over the rock-paved streets most excruciatingly. The foot climb was preferable, and we were young."

Coolbrith, after whom the little park atop Russian Hill is named, hosted literary gatherings at her house at 1067 Broadway with the likes of Bret Harte and Charles Warren Stoddard. Another charismatic woman, Kate Atkinson, held bohemian dinner parties at her still standing 1853 house at 1032 Broadway, attracting guests such as bad-boy architect and fellow Russian Hill dweller Willis Polk and two inseparable pals who were to write their names into Russian Hill lore: writer Gelett Burgess, the dandy who took the goat trail to avoid the young Italian toughs, and artist and designer Bruce Porter, who helped design the Rock House.

Burgess was a respectable Bostonian teaching topographical drawing at the University of California–Berkeley in 1894 when he punched his one-way ticket to Bohemia by enlisting Porter and two other friends in a madcap prank, toppling a statue of a teetotaling dentist named Henry Cogswell. UC found out and fired Burgess, whereupon he gave up his modern apartment at Green and Leavenworth and moved two blocks to a dilapidated house on the summit of Russian Hill.

There was "no queerer, quainter, crookeder a house, nor a house in worse array, of more tatterdemalion an aspect and cock-sided disrepute than the chunk of queer cottage at No. 1031 Vallejo Street," he wrote.

Burgess and Porter proceeded to publish two madcap little magazines, the *Lark* and *Le Petit Journal des Refusées*, which delighted readers and critics with their irreverence and lightheartedness. The two friends were often seen walking from the hill's summit down the goat path to the "Lower Town." A diminutive man known as "the Walking Peanut," Burgess wore a long cape with a Wildean carnation; the lanky Porter dressed in black. They remained friends for more than sixty years. Porter married the daughter of philosopher William James, and the couple hosted their own intellectual salons at their house at 944 Chestnut Street. Poet George Sterling, known as the "King of Bohemia," haunted the hill's lanes before making the ultimate bohemian exit, killing himself by taking cyanide in his room at the Bohemian Club. Other noteworthy writers who lived on the hill were Helen Hunt Jackson, Will Irwin, and Lucia Chamberlain.

Bohemia has mostly fled the multimillion-dollar precincts of Russian Hill, but there is at least one holdout. The illustrious ninety-six-year-old novelist Herb Gold—who happens to have written a book on bohemias—still lives on Broadway near the hill's summit, in the same apartment he has occupied since the 1950s. It is a pleasure to report that Gold's apartment is queer, quaint, crooked, and tatterdemalion.

# CHAPTER 16

# SOUTH PARK

## GEORGE GORDON'S EXCLUSIVE OVAL

ONCE YOU START learning about a city's history, every neighborhood starts to feel like Dr. Jekyll and Mr. Hyde. The ritziest part of town turns out to have been a garbage dump, the worst slum a debutante's backyard. Even streets can have embarrassing pasts: elegant Green Street was named after a con man from Philadelphia named Talbot Green, who was an esteemed San Francisco citizen until a woman from back home recognized him as a grifter. But some places have more schizophrenic histories than others. And the area that has witnessed the most extreme swings in all of San Francisco is a peculiar little oval off Bryant and Second streets called South Park.

South Park was created in the instant city's early days by a hard-driving British immigrant named George Gordon. Gordon had organized an association of forty-niners and taken the unusual Nicaragua route to California, which proved fortuitous: the lumber he purchased there was the foundation of his fortune. After establishing one of the city's first iron foundries, the Vulcan Iron Works, in 1852 Gordon began buying up lots between Bryant and Brannan and Second and Third streets. Here Gordon planned to create the city's first luxury residential development and private park.

It was a shrewd choice. At the time, most of the city's wealthy inhabitants lived around Stockton and Washington streets, in what is now Chinatown, but the increasing proximity of prostitutes made that area undesirable. However, they had few places to move. Most of the town was covered with sand dunes, the three downtown hills were difficult to climb or build on, and much of the South of Market area was a swamp. In this restricted geography, South Park—described at the time as "the only level spot free of sand in the city's limits"—was a beckoning, flat oasis. It was fairly close to the city's heart around Montgomery Street. And it was also just south of Rincon Hill—then an actual hill—upon which a few nabobs had begun building mansions.

Gordon modeled South Park on aristocratic English spaces such as Berkeley Square, with large houses built around a private oval-shaped park. The oval was 550 feet long and enclosed by an ornamental locked fence. An 1856 photograph shows a formal gate with two elegant stone pillars on the east side of the oval; an imposing row of mansions lines the northwest edge of the park, with a large wind-mill in the center, used for pumping water for the lawn. The first seventeen houses were handsome two-story brick structures, built with clay obtained when the basements of the houses were excavated. The kitchen, dining room, and servants' quarters were in the basement, various parlors on the first floor, and bedrooms (generally five) on the second.

An economic downturn in 1855 slowed sales, and Gordon never made much money on his venture. Still, many wealthy and prominent San Franciscans bought mansions or lots in South Park, including grain king Isaac Friedlander, future Wells Fargo president Lloyd Tevis, Pacific Mail shipping executive Commodore Watkins, railroad magnate David D. Colton, and U.S. senator William Gwin. South Park and Rincon Hill quickly became the new city's one and only patrician quarter. San Francisco's first social register, the *Elite Directory* of 1879, asserted, "There was little that was stylish and correct in the city except in its vicinity . . . South Park became noted for its kettledrums, balls, and Germans."

"Kettledrums"—informal ladies' afternoon teas—balls, parties, and lavish din-ners were a specialty of the Gwins and the many other wealthy southerners who lived in South Park or Rincon Hill. The oyster suppers and eggnog receptions at the Gwins' were famous.

In the 1860s and 1870s, the custom of New Year's calling reached the height of its popularity. "Battalions of young men dashed about from house to house to be greeted by a chorus of young women who immediately took them to tables groaning under vast displays of hot fish, cold birds, jellied meats, salads and desserts," a society writer for the *Chronicle* recalled. "Dinners began at 6:30 and lasted until midnight, course after course coming slowly but surely at the festive board."

But South Park was only a haven for San Francisco's Four Hundred for about twenty years. The explosive growth of industry in the surrounding South of Market neighborhood, and a catastrophically ill-advised municipal "improvement," sent it into a downward spiral from which it would not pull out for more than a century.

## THE UNKINDEST CUT

Today, Rincon Hill is a truncated stub. But during the heyday of South Park, it was a real hill, the main geographic feature for miles around, marking the southern end of Yerba Buena Cove just as Telegraph Hill marked its north. At its summit, near Second Street and Harrison, it was close to one hundred feet high. Its bay views, good weather, and proximity to downtown made it, along with adjoining South Park, the most sought-after place to live in the young city. In the 1850s and 1860s, opulent wooden mansions with beautiful gardens lined Harrison, Bryant, and Second and small cross streets such as Essex and Hawthorne. It was a veritable oasis of verdant elegance.

Two things led to the downfall of Rincon Hill and adjoining South Park. First, factories and other industries poured into South of Market, bringing pollution, noise, and crowds of working-class people with whom the aristocrats did not wish to rub shoulders. As an 1892 article in the *Chronicle* noted, "There was no way of reaching Rincon Hill without traversing this section, which soon became known as 'Tar Flat,' and almost as soon as it reached its zenith of glory decadence set in. Another quarter was selected, property values fell, and Rincon Hill became the tawdry, shabby-genteel locality that it is now."

The second thing that brought Rincon Hill down—literally—was one of the most notorious terrain alterations in the city's history: the Second Street Cut. The man responsible for this profanation of San Francisco's landscape was a real estate speculator named John Middleton. In 1868, Middleton—who had managed to get himself elected to the state assembly for this very purpose—proposed a state bill requiring the city to cut through Rincon Hill at Second Street, two blocks northeast of South Park. Harrison would be lowered eighty-seven feet, and a wooden bridge built over the chasm. This Second Street Cut, as it became known, would allow heavy teams to go back and forth between downtown and the Pacific Mail wharves on Brannan Street. Middleton was convinced this would stimulate commerce in South Beach and make the city more attractive as a railroad terminus. (He also owned a large lot on Second and Bryant and stood to profit from the deal.)

Many San Franciscans—especially the nabobs living on Rincon Hill and in South Park—were horrified. They protested that the Second Street Cut would slice out the center of Rincon Hill and leave many houses—including some of the finest ones in the city—clinging to the edge of a cliff. "Prominent gentlemen . . . will look down on their residences, tottering on the brink of a precipice," the *Alta* editorialized, waggishly adding, "May we never have to write their epitaphs, 'How the mighty have fallen.'"

But other residents supported the cut, arguing that progress required it, that the interests of a few wealthy citizens should not take precedence over the welfare of the entire city, and that real estate values in the area would soar. The *Alta* changed its tune, insisting that "public necessity demanded" the cut and proudly proclaiming, "We have done more in a score of years in changing the topography of the city than Venice did in five centuries or Amsterdam in two, and those cities, like ours, were built up partly in defiance of nature."

The critics' protests were in vain. In 1869, 250 teams of horses and five hundred men began hauling away Rincon Hill. The result was a complete debacle. As the historian J. S. Hittell wrote in 1878, "The work was done, but the predicted benefits failed to make their appearance. The cut or ditch, at one place sixty feet deep, has ugly steep banks, which have slid down in wet weather; the falling dirt has destroyed the sidewalks; the despoiled lot owners have refused to keep the pavement in repair; heavy teams have found it more convenient to pass through other streets in going to and coming from the Pacific Mail wharf; Rincon Hill has lost much of its beauty and all its pre-eminence as a district for fashionable buildings; the most active advocates of the scheme made nothing by it; and the direct expense of the improvement was $385,000, while the loss to citizens beyond all benefits was not less than one million dollars. Many had to pay for the errors of judgment committed by a few."

"Many a fair Rincon Hill garden and home was hung suspended like Mahomet's coffin high in air," a *Chronicle* reporter wrote in 1917. "It was a ghastly wound and the huge, unsightly bridge over Second Street did not improve the mise en scene, by any means. It was a heartrending sight to see the remnant of a once beautiful garden hanging over the mutilated hillside or a fragment of a summer house or part of a kitchen trying to balance themselves on the brink."

Soon after the cut was completed, a British parson called on Bishop Kip, who was living at 348 Second Street. He wrote, "[I] found in the part where his house ought to have been a fresh-made cliff, 50 feet high, on either side, and a crowd of navies carting away stuff. It was impossible to reach the Bishop's nest from the street, so I beat round to get to the back of it. On arriving at the spot I asked where the Bishop lived. 'The Bishop?' said a jolly-looking gentleman to me; 'why, his house tumbled down into the street.'"

Even without the Second Street Cut, Rincon Hill and South Park would not have lasted long as the city's fashionable districts. By the 1870s, they were elegant islands surrounded by a rising sea of industry and tenements—the very things, as some observers did not fail to point out, that had made their inhabitants rich. But the cut, combined with the invention of the cable car, finished them off. Society moved to now accessible Nob Hill and later to the Western Addition. By the 1890s, only a few names in the Blue Book, the city's social register, were listed with Rincon or South Park addresses. Robert Louis Stevenson explored the area in 1892 and wrote, "I had discovered a new slum, a place of precarious sandy cliffs, deep sandy cuttings, solitary ancient houses and butt ends of streets."

The 1906 earthquake and fire destroyed the few remnants of Rincon Hill's and South Park's golden age. Today, Rincon Hill itself is barely recognizable as a hill, obscured by the anchorage to the Bay Bridge and a sleek, towering high-rise—the latter a return, albeit a far less elegant one, to the neighborhood's upper-crust origins.

## THE EARTHQUAKE TENEMENTS

The 1906 earthquake and fire, the worst disaster ever to befall an American city, killed more than three thousand people and destroyed almost all of the city between the Embarcadero and Van Ness Avenue, along with the South of Market region and much of the Mission District. Two hundred and fifty thousand people were left homeless.

In the immediate aftermath of the catastrophe, relief workers set up tent villages in parks and squares. These served a temporary need, but by summer, with the rainy season approaching, officials realized they needed to provide more substantial shelter, particularly for working-class residents. Disproportionately Irish and Italian, these workers lived mostly South of Market and in North Beach. The city feared that if they didn't have decent housing, they would leave the city.

To house San Francisco's working poor, the city's main relief organization began building small wooden cottages, popularly called "earthquake shacks." These cottages came in two- and three-room models, cost about $150 to build,

measured either ten by eighteen feet or ten by fourteen feet, and were painted park-bench green. The 5,610 earthquake shacks were built and set up in lines in twenty-six official camps, located in parks and squares across the city, from Washington Square to the Presidio to Golden Gate Park to Lobos Square to Dolores Park.

One, and only one, city-owned open space featured a different type of earthquake-relief structure: South Park. Authorities decided that the tiny oval was too small to accommodate a cottage camp. But earthquake housing in the area was desperately needed: after Chinatown, South of Market was the poorest and most densely populated part of the city. Accordingly, relief officials decided to build nineteen two-story tenements in South Park, along with a one-story bathhouse and laundry building.

The *San Francisco Relief Survey*, published in 1913, describes the South Park tenements. "Some of the buildings were divided into 16 suites of 2 rooms each and the others into 12 tenements of two rooms each. The total number of rooms was 656. The maximum population was 648. They had adequate fire protection and the occupants were required to take part regularly in a fire drill. There was steady demand for the rooms, by reason of the nearness of the camp to the shipping and manufacturing districts. The tenements were full almost all the time."

In addition to housing, relief organizations provided social workers to work with the city's needy. They were particularly needed in poor South Park, which was home to the first "settlement house" in San Francisco, established by the pioneering reformer Jane Addams after she visited the city in 1894. A miniature version of her famous Hull House in Chicago, the South Park Settlement House, located at 15 South Park, was started by idealistic college students and professors from Berkeley and Stanford.

The settlement movement was a fascinating example of early American social activism. Its middle-class and upper-class supporters—who were mostly young and often described as being interested in "sociology"—aspired to help working-class people by providing them with access to services of all kinds, including sewing, sports, lectures on cultural, political, and intellectual themes, advice on how to mother, and so on. In keeping with one of Addams's core beliefs, some of the students lived in the house, whose $45 rent was paid by Phoebe Apperson Hearst, wife of the mining magnate, mother of the famous publisher, and one of the city's great philanthropists. They were determined not to be patronizing toward the poor people they worked with and insisted that they learned as much from them as vice versa. All four of the city's settlement houses, including the Telegraph Hill Neighborhood Association and the Columbia Park Boys' Club, were destroyed by the fire, and earthquake-relief social workers tried to fill the void.

South Park's tenements, like most of the refugee camps, were open for a little longer than a year, from December 3, 1906, to January 7, 1908. Most of the earthquake shacks were salvaged and hauled away by their occupants after they were ordered removed from the parks and squares, but the South Park tenements met a different fate. Five were sold at auction; the rest were broken down (an early example of modular housing, they were constructed in such a way that they could be taken apart and reassembled) and moved to the property on which the new Almshouse was being built, where they served as administration buildings. The Almshouse, which served the city's poor and elderly, was eventually replaced by Laguna Honda Hospital, and the old wooden tenements were presumably razed. A number of earthquake shacks can still be found around San Francisco (particularly in Bernal Heights), but the nineteen tenements of South Park have vanished without a trace.

# A JAPANTOWN SOUTH OF MARKET

Almost forgotten among the almost psychedelic transformations that South Park has gone through is the fact that it was one of San Francisco's first two Japantowns. The earliest Japanese immigrants, who arrived in 1869, mostly settled in Chinatown, but their numbers were never great enough to constitute a distinct community. Later nineteenth-century arrivals lived mostly in the working-class South of Market area. The first two real Nihonmachis (Japantowns) sprang up after the earthquake—one in the Western Addition, where Japantown is now, the other in South Park.

From 1906 to the mid-1930s, thousands of Japanese—including both first-generation immigrants (issei) and Japanese visitors—lived in more than half a dozen Japanese-owned hotels and rooming houses on the north side of the park. The biggest hotel was the Bo Chow at 102 South Park; others included the Kumamoto at 70 South Park, the Eimoto at 22–24, the Kinokumiya at 84, the Omiya at 104–106, and the Higoya. Japanese businessmen also owned a grocery store and souvenir shop at 108–110 South Park, as well as the Biwako Baths.

Arriving Japanese were drawn to South Park because it was only two blocks from the Pacific Mail docks, where steamers from Japan landed, and two blocks

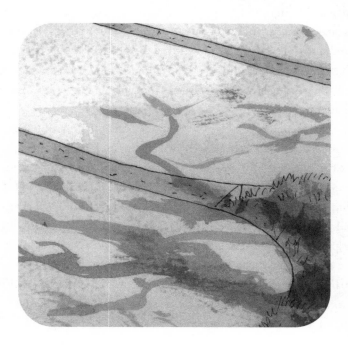

from the Southern Pacific Railroad station. Japanese would disembark from the ships and go directly to the Bo Chow or other Japanese hotels on South Park. For thirty years, San Francisco newspapers regularly featured classified ads placed by Japanese seeking domestic employment as houseboys and chauffeurs, among other positions.

The owner of the Bo Chow hotel, E. T. Arima, was a leader in the Japanese community. In 1930, he had been a resident of San Francisco for twenty-six years, was educated in American schools, and held a law degree. Arima was president of the Japan Hotel Association of San Francisco, the Japanese Men's Club, and many other organizations.

Despite—in some cases because of—the presence of successful middle-class figures such as Arima, San Franciscans in general regarded Japanese with even more suspicion and hostility than they did the Chinese. In 1916, one S. Nakahara applied for a permit to erect two Japanese gateways, remnants of the Japan Beautiful exhibit at the just closed Panama-Pacific International Exposition, in South Park, but anti-Japanese sentiment led the park commissioners to reject the plan. The fact that South Park became heavily Japanese after the earthquake indicates how far the once patrician quarter had sunk.

South Park's Japantown lasted about thirty years. Its population was frozen when Japanese immigration was outlawed in 1924, and the coup de grâce came a few years later, when Japanese shipping companies moved their piers north of the Ferry Building. The construction of the Bay Bridge wiped out its last remnants. In the 1930s, the Japanese residents of South Park and other areas moved to the Western Addition, where they established a much larger Nihonmachi around Post and Buchanan streets.

South Park was never exclusively Japanese. After the earthquake, a number of Filipinos also moved there, as well as working-class whites. In 1921, Filipino merchant marines and others pooled their money and bought the Omiya hotel at 104–106 South Park, renaming it the Gran Oriente Filipino Hotel. This hotel served Filipino seamen and, remarkably, did not close until 2008. Filipinos also purchased two more apartment buildings, at 41–43 and 45–49 South Park. On the latter parcel they built the Gran Oriente Filipino Masonic Temple, which is still active and became the nucleus of the city's Filipino community.

After the Japanese left, large numbers of African Americans moved into South Park. Ironically, exactly the same demographic transformation took place in Japantown just a few years later, when blacks who had come to San Francisco to work in the wartime shipyards moved into homes vacated by Japanese who had been forcibly removed—or, in the official parlance, "relocated"—to prison camps. Both situations were made possible because at the time South Park and the Western Addition were deemed undesirable by middle-class whites, so minorities were allowed to move in and eventually to succeed each other.

## A HISTORY IN CRIME, PART ONE: 1865–1888

A fascinating way of tracing South Park's strange and convoluted history is by looking at the crimes committed there. The (noncomprehensive) list in the following three sections was obtained by searching under "South Park" in the online archives of the *San Francisco Chronicle*. All quoted passages are from the *Chronicle*.

During South Park's aristocratic heyday, from 1855 to around 1875, there was, not surprisingly, very little crime. In fact, there is no mention of any criminal activity from 1865 to 1880, with the exception of two stories in 1871 and 1875. During the depressed 1870s the neighborhood, like other parts of San Francisco, was troubled by a new phenomenon: "hoodlums," young working-class toughs, many of Irish ancestry, who were America's first juvenile delinquents.

**AUGUST 15, 1871.** John Riley stabbed F. P. Coakley as he entered his house in South Park about three A.M. Sunday morning. Coakley was arrested and held on a charge of assault to commit murder, with bail set at $1,000.

**OCTOBER 7, 1871.** "The citizens of South Park are greatly annoyed by the hideous yells of 'night hawks' and pilfering by original Hoodlums, who it is said congregate there in large numbers, and have not lost any of their old audacity and fearlessness. This gang should be broken up immediately."

**MARCH 23, 1875.** Two men who participated in the hoodlum disturbance at South Park on Saturday were convicted of disturbing the peace and vulgar language.

By the 1880s, many of South Park's luxurious mansions had been turned into boardinghouses, and more crimes began to be reported.

JANUARY 10, 1884. Two men were arrested at one A.M. at the rear of 40 South Park by two police officers who heard the sound of a boarder's pistol. James Brady and William McLaughlin were caught with a sack containing five chickens and a turkey.

JUNE 29, 1886. A female customs inspector was arrested for smuggling opium into her residence at 330 Brannan, which had a South Park entrance.

Because South Park was privately owned until 1895, when the owners gave it to the city, the police did not patrol it.

JANUARY 25, 1888. "Within the past year a number of residents of the Park have been 'held up' and relieved of their valuables . . . One resident of South Park told the Chronicle that about 10 nights ago, when returning home, he was pounced upon by a footpad and only that he carried a heavy cane with which he held the robber at bay, he might have been seriously wounded." When residents complained to Sergeant Falls of the Southern Police Station, he replied, "There is no beat that takes in South Park. The officers patrol Bryant and Brannan streets, 2nd and 3rd, but they are not supposed to take in South Park. Of course, should a cry for help come from that locality the officers would run there."

## A HISTORY IN CRIME, PART TWO: 1889–1903

By the 1890s, only a few wealthy families remained in South Park, which had become a tough, working-class South of Market neighborhood.

JUNE 18, 1891. A man named Patrick Clark forced his little boy to go door-to-door in South Park begging for money, which the father would use for drink. The boy said they were homeless and lay down "wherever night overtook them." He often slept in hallways while his father was in a saloon.

APRIL 28, 1893. Two millers at the Del Monte mills were accused of corrupting schoolchildren. David H. Sweet and George E. Williams were arrested for having obscene literature in their South Park room and on their persons. They were charged with "the atrocious practice of distributing vile circulars and pamphlets to the boys and girls who attend the public schools south of Market Street."

**MARCH 3, 1895.** "Gerlach's cheap chimney." Fred Gerlach and seven youngsters were arrested for tearing up fifteen feet of the low brick wall surrounding South Park. Gerlach intended to use the bricks to make a chimney at his nearby home. They were charged with malicious mischief.

**AUGUST 18, 1896.** A middle-aged woman who gave her name as Kate Gavin was arrested for theft. She entered the room of Mary Presko at 16 South Park and stole $65, then stashed it in a Howard Street saloon.

**FEBRUARY 28, 1897.** Mollie Hagan, daughter of the leader of the Baldwin Orchestra and a former Alameda debutante, stabbed her husband, John, a marine fireman, to death at their room in a lodging house at 33 South Park with a carving knife. The couple quarreled frequently, and she claimed he had come at her with an ax.

The surest indication that South Park had fallen on hard times was the arrival of freelance writers.

**FEBRUARY 19, 1898.** John J. Livernash, 60 South Park, committed suicide in a saloon by stabbing himself in the chest. "His friends state that he had endeavored to sell an article to a morning paper, and failing, had become morose and greatly depressed."

**AUGUST 27, 1898.** An ex-con named George Wood hit sailor Charles Miller over the head with a slung shot (a blackjack) in a robbery attempt in South Park. But Miller was not stunned and held on to Wood until the police came.

**SEPTEMBER 29, 1901.** A nine-month-old girl and a three-year-old boy were found at the home of Mr. and Mrs. Ruffner at 144 South Park. They had been left alone for six or seven hours and were crying piteously. The children were taken to the Hall of Justice police matron.

**DECEMBER 2, 1901.** South Park resident Johnnie O'Keefe, thirteen, hit Patrick Carr, who peddled sheet music on the corner of Market and Third streets, with a missile from a rubber slingshot. Carr was in danger of losing the sight in his right eye. O'Keefe was charged with attempted murder.

**FEBRUARY 10, 1903.** Mrs. O'Keefe of 115 South Park asked the court to commit her seventeen-year-old son, Andrew, to reform school because of his dissolute habits. She told the court, "Her boy was not right and had become a member of a gang of juvenile hoodlums and petty thieves." Judge Lawlor was to commit the boy to the Whittier (reform) School the next day.

## A HISTORY IN CRIME, PART THREE: 1903–1936

The temporary earthquake tenements in South Park were the targets of crime. Later, the neighborhood's new Japanese, Filipino, and African American arrivals joined whites on the police blotter.

**JULY 8, 1907.** Carpenter Chester Campbell, who was living in a refugee cottage in South Park with his two young sons, was arrested for trying to burn down 53 Sterling Place.

**NOVEMBER 8, 1907.** A sneak thief burglarized the earthquake tenements, entering apartment H9, where he stole $84 and a watch, then B12, where he took $4.

**DECEMBER 25, 1907.** John Drinkhouse's cigar factory on South Park was robbed of two cases of cigars worth $700. The suspects were "4 apparent Mexicans."

**APRIL 17, 1909.** Tomijo Kawamoto, a deserting Japanese sailor from the ship *Chiyo Maru*, was shot and killed by a policeman at Second and South Park after he lunged at the officer with a knife.

**AUGUST 20, 1910.** John Hartmann, proprietor of a saloon at 516 Second Street, was charged with assault with a deadly weapon after he clubbed George Glober, who lived in a shack on South Park, during a quarrel.

**JUNE 7, 1921.** A Japanese rancher named N. Nakakuma sued Z. Shiozaki, the owner of the Kinokumiya Hotel, for $25,000 damages. Nakakuma and his wife, Toshi, arrived from Japan on April 20 and checked into the hotel. Nakakuma alleged that when he was out, Shiozaki criminally attacked his wife, who went insane as a result and subsequently died.

**MARCH 14, 1926.** Two men got into an argument in front of a house at 26 South Park. When a third man tried to make peace, a three-way razor fight broke out. Angelo Mendoza had most of his scalp cut away, and Marcus Romero and Louis Cubrillos were badly cut. All lived at 11 de Boom Street.

**OCTOBER 19, 1926.** Police raided a top-floor apartment at 47 South Park, home of the notorious "terror bandit" Clarence Kelly Jr., twenty-two, who with two accomplices killed four people in cold blood during a two-night murder and robbery spree. As Kelly ran into a neighbor's apartment, police opened fire, almost killing two innocent women. The wounded Kelly, a former boxer and taxi driver, was found hiding in a bedroom closet. He was sent to San Quentin, where his father was also imprisoned, and later executed.

**JANUARY 2, 1929.** During a New Year's celebration, three men stabbed Rodarefo Orszo in front of 41 South Park. Seeking revenge, Orszo set three fires in a building at 43 South Park. Weakened by loss of blood, he crawled to Third and Bryant, where he pulled the fire alarm. Firemen put out the fire. His condition was serious.

**MAY 12, 1929.** In his apartment at 41 South Park—apparently a violence-prone building—Ignacio Aguelera shot and killed his friend Louis Pineda and wounded his wife, Natalia, in the shoulder when he found them together after he returned home from work. He then stepped into the street and fatally shot himself in the head.

**FEBRUARY 10, 1930.** Mrs. Stella Lometti, forty-nine, who lived in a rooming house at 90 South Park, was taken to a hospital where she died of complications of alcoholism after a prolonged rum-drinking bout with her partner, fifty-year-old Fred G. Kammerer. Kammerer also died when fractured ribs caused by an earlier fight, which he was apparently too drunk to be aware of, perforated his lungs.

**JANUARY 26, 1932.** Helen Small, forty, of 26 South Park, "a negress," stabbed a policeman when he went to question her about a burglary.

**JULY 4, 1934 (THE BIG WATERFRONT STRIKE).** "In South Park, there were furious melees between gangs of strikers and small detachments of police. Clubs, guns and tear gas drove them out of this area eventually, but from South Park came at least six casualties so serious as to require hospital treatment."

**MAY 19, 1936.** "Albert Jackson, 53, a Negro, was shot and critically wounded yesterday when he tried to escape from Federal Narcotics Officer George H. White in an alley near 76A South Park street. White took nine Negro women and five Negro men into custody as material witnesses. They were held at Southern station as $1000 vagrants." In a peculiar coincidence, trigger-happy narcotics officer George Hunter White was later a major player in one of the most bizarre schemes in the history of the CIA. Starting in 1955, White monitored a top-secret CIA mind-control experiment in San Francisco called Operation Midnight Climax. Hired prostitutes would lure unsuspecting johns from North Beach bars to a cheesily-furnished safe house on Chestnut Street known as "the pad," dose them with LSD, and have sex with them. White, sitting on a portable toilet behind a two-way mirror and quaffing martinis from a pitcher he kept in a refrigerator, would observe the X-rated proceedings to see if the dosed men would reveal secrets. The pad was not shuttered until 1965.

**JANUARY 20, 1936.** A twenty-nine-year-old seaman, trying to commit suicide at a hotel at 126 South Park, set off a gas explosion.

## THE BONFIRE

Of all the odd things that have taken place in South Park during its long, strange history, the oddest—and, in a way, the most poetically fitting—may have been the great bonfire.

From the 1930s until the 1960s, a big bonfire burned more or less continually in the center of South Park. The bonfire started in the days when the park was home to large numbers of longshoremen, who would stand around it and warm themselves while waiting for early morning calls from the Union Hall. Originally it was fed with trash and construction debris. As the neighborhood deteriorated, the city was forced to provide fuel for the bonfire because poor and homeless men had begun to tear apart abandoned buildings to use as firewood. By the 1970s, South Park had been largely taken over by the homeless, the mentally ill, and drug users, and eventually the fire was banned.

By a peculiar twist of fate, the first time I came upon South Park, on a late afternoon in 1972, a fire was burning in a trash can, surrounded by five or six old black men. I don't think it was the same fire, because the fabled bonfire that started in the 1930s was located in the center of the park, and the one I saw was on the west end, near Third Street. Nor was it really a bonfire. But it was still a fire.

I did not learn about the great bonfire of South Park until I was writing this book, almost half a century after I first stumbled upon the hidden oval. I had come unknowingly in at the end of the last, smoldering chapter of an old story.

That trash can fire, and the old men who were gathered around it, are long gone. South Park has become a wealthy enclave once again, a hip South of Market gathering place for techies and designers. But this upturn in South Park's fortunes happened before, during the first dot-com boom in 1999, and then everything turned to ashes again. So it is unwise to assume anything is permanent here.

Except ghosts. For every now and then, when a gust of wind blows a yellowing leaf along one of the old oval's walkways, or a certain slant of light falls upon a weathered building, South Park opens itself to the mystery of the past, and all the people who lived and worked and laughed and were born and died here—the forty-niners and bankers and longshoremen and Japanese and Filipinos and blacks and Mexicans and Swedes and students and Irish and sailors and clerks and servants and hotelkeepers and housemaids—appear again, like smoky wraiths that dance and flicker in the only bonfire that never goes out, the bonfire of time.

# ACKNOWLEDGMENTS

In 2013, I was approached by Bloomsbury to make a series of drawings for a book called *Cool Gray City of Love*. The author was someone I had heard of, but not met, Gary Kamiya. His essays were a wonderful mix of history and personal reflection, and with the subtitle of *49 Views of San Francisco*, how could I not be interested? Problem was, I only had a month to make the drawings. At the time, my series All Over Coffee was running in the *San Francisco Chronicle*. For the first two years I'd been publishing four days a week, but by this time I'd slowed the pace to weekly in order to work on other projects. Still, even with my ability for high output, I couldn't do forty-nine drawings in that short of a time; or at least not to the caliber I would have liked. So, despite my desire to work on the project, I had to pass. I sent a note to Gary, expressing my regret.

A couple years later, Gary and I were being honored by the Northern California Book Awards and had a chance to meet. We instantly hit it off. It was one of those circumstances where within minutes you find yourself laughing together as if you were old friends. We both lamented that we had been unable to work together on *Cool Gray City* and agreed that one day we would find the right project.

A few more years passed. I had ended All Over Coffee and was immersed in launching my career as a novelist. For a while I'd been happy to be free of the weekly deadline, which I had adhered to for twelve years, but after publishing a novel that had taken me six years, the thought of returning to short pieces felt like relief. I had rented a new studio space and committed to two years of focusing on large drawings. Coincidentally, the day I was moving, I received a call from the *Chronicle*'s former art director, Matt Petty. He was now art director at the *Nob Hill Gazette* and asked if I was interested in starting a new series. The timing was impeccable.

In May of 2018, the *Gazette* launched Quotable City, a monthly series that paired trivia and quotes from famous figures to historic San Francisco sites. The series was fun and unlike anything I had done before, but the research was overwhelming. At one point I had both an intern and an assistant, and even then, finalizing the text was taking longer than the drawings, several of which were as large as four by five feet.

In a short time, the work became too much and I knew I needed to close the book on Quotable City. I was enjoying the routine of regular publishing again, though. It was helping my productivity, even with the next novel, which I had also begun. So before giving up on the series I sat down to retool, and that's when I thought of Gary.

I instantly knew that collaborating with such a naturally obsessive history lover would be a perfect balance, but I didn't want to continue with the same premise as Quotable City. If Gary was to collaborate as a writer, his contribution needed to be 100 percent his own. It was how it would have had to have been for me, so it was only fair to structure the partnership that way. I invited Gary to my studio and pitched us working together, but not just on the series for the *Gazette*. My idea was that we would also make a book. By having a monthly publishing schedule, we could work out our ideas, find our form, and gauge audience feedback, then, in a year, we would have all the makings to pitch a book.

Gary loved the idea, and within weeks we had the outline of what would become our new monthly series, Spirits of the City. The *Gazette* gave us the green light, and in April 2019, Spirits made its debut. Less than a year later, we had a book deal. From the moment we began—from sitting in cafes crossing off possible titles, to driving around the city scouting, to being surrounded by a team of heavies who chased us off a construction site we had snuck onto—Gary and I worked together effortlessly. It's rare that a partnership or a plan, especially creative, goes so smoothly, but I'm proud—and lucky—to say that it would be hard to imagine a more affable and well-matched collaborator. Some of it is because both Gary and I have been around the block and back again working for print, and some of it is because we both love San Francisco and have found a genuine kinship with the city as our muse, but mainly it's because we each have a profound respect for the other's talents, and simply get along well.

So while this book is a celebration of San Francisco's deliciously sorted past and endlessly drawable vistas, it's also a celebration of good collaboration—and not just between Gary and me. Each step of this project has proven to be a pleasure, and I would like to thank everyone who worked with us to get here: Erin Carlson, Matt Petty, and the *Nob Hill Gazette*; Eva Jewett-Gatschet and Judi Leff; Erin Carew and Peter Sullivan; Ellen Levine and Trident Media Group; Nancy Miller, Elizabeth Ellis, Akshaya Iyer, Rosie Mahorter, and Laura Phillips at Bloomsbury; and my wife, Joen Madonna. Thank you. I would also like to thank everyone who has purchased this book, and everyone who shares a love of this magical, sometimes frustrating, and always beautiful city. Despite the obvious lack of people in my drawings, without us wacky inhabitants and our crazy ideas, San Francisco would not be the spirited city it is.

Paul Madonna, July 2020

I'VE GREATLY BENEFITED from conversations and correspondence with many fellow toilers in the vast vineyard of San Francisco history, including Gray Brechin, Chris Carlsson, Robert Cherny, John Freeman, Herbert Gold, Michael Johns, Woody LaBounty, Katherine Petrin, Jimmie Schein, Peter Stein, David Talbot, and Jim Yager. Western Neighborhoods Project founders Woody LaBounty and David Gallagher's website Outside Lands, and Chris Carlsson's website Found SF, have been valuable resources. Special thanks to the helpful and friendly staff at the most valuable resource of all, the San Francisco History Center at the San Francisco Library.

Gary Kamiya, July 2020

# SELECTED BIBLIOGRAPHY

## CHAPTER ONE: JOICE STREET

Information on the Lower Nob Hill Apartment Hotel District is found in the nomination document for the National Register of Historic Places (online).

Dashiell Hammett's footprints in San Francisco are described in The Dashiell Hammett Tour by Don Herron. The effect of the 1766 "Hat and Cloak Riots" in Madrid on Carlos III's decision to expel the Jesuits is discussed in "French Influence and the Origins of the Bourbon Colonial Reorganization" by Allen J. Kuethe and Lowell Blaisdell, an article that appeared in *The Hispanic American Historical Review*, August 1991. The ramshackle shantytown that stood atop Nob Hill during the city's early years is described in Charles Lockwood's *Suddenly San Francisco: The Early Years of an Instant City*. The information about Erastus Joice was obtained from the Fern Hill Times website, written by Hudson Bell, historian of the Nob Hill Association. https://fernhilltoursdotcom.wordpress.com/2013/03/19/the-truth-about-joice-street-the-man-it-was-named-for-erastus-volney-joice/ The quote about the good-natured Joice hunting is from *Men and Memories of San Francisco, in the "Spring of '50"* by T. A. Barry and B. A. Patten. The Andrew Hallidie sections are largely based on "Hallidie's Folly: The Story of the Clay Street Hill Railroad Cable Cars" by Michael Phipps, an article that appeared in the winter 2009 issue of *The Argonaut*. The story of the first woman to ride a cable car is from a contemporaneous account in the *San Francisco Chronicle*. Donaldina Cameron's harrowing first rescue mission is recounted in *Chinatown's Angry Angel: The Story of Donaldina Cameron*, by Mildred Crowl Martin. *The White Devil's Daughters: The Women Who Fought Slavery in San Francisco's Chinatown*, by Julia Flynn Siler, describes the key role played by Tien Fu Wu. Information on the contemporary Cameron House was obtained by an author interview with Cameron House staff.

# CHAPTER TWO: PIER 24

*The Ferry Building: Witness to a Century of Change* and *Vanished Waters: A History of San Francisco's Mission Bay,* both by Nancy Olmsted, discuss the history of the port. The atmosphere of the Embarcadero in its shipping heyday is described in *San Francisco in the 1930s: The WPA Guide to the City by the Bay.* The statistics on cargo weight handled by longshoremen are found in "Cargo Handling and Longshore Labor Conditions" by Boris Stern, Bulletin #550 of the U.S. Bureau of Labor Statistics (1932). The 1926 report on cargo handled by the port is quoted in the description of the Embarcadero in the National Register of Historic Places (https://sfport.com/embarcadero-historic-district). The piers are discussed in Michael Corbett's *Port City: The History and Transformation of the Port of San Francisco, 1848–2010.*

Charles Nelson's life is recounted in "Sea Captains: San Francisco 1880s" on the Maritime History Project website: https://www.maritimeheritage.org/captains/nelsonCharles.html

The section on the coastwise shipping industry is based on Giles Brown's "The Culmination and Decline of Pacific Castwise Shipping, 1916–1936," which appeared in the July 1949 *Pacific Northwest Quarterly.* The story about Thomas Fleming working on the *Emma Alexander* is related on this National Park Service website: https://www.nps.gov/safr/learn/historyculture/thomasfleming.htm

# CHAPTER THREE: DIVISION STREET

Happy Valley is discussed in *Rincon Hill and South Park: San Francisco's Early Fashionable Neighborhood* by Albert Shumate. San Francisco's "hobohemia" is described in Alvin Averbach's "San Francisco's South of Market District 1850–1860: The Emergence of a Skid Row," which appeared in the Fall 1973 California Historical Quarterly. Dumpville is discussed in two Portals of the Past San Francisco history columns by this author that appeared in the *San Francisco Chronicle* on October 16 and 23, 2015 (https://www.sfchronicle.com/bayarea/article/Big-homeless-camp-today-near-S-F-s-old-6574857.php; https://www.sfchronicle.com/bayarea/article/Life-among-the-trash-the-rise-and-fall-of-6587303.php).

# CHAPTER FOUR: THE TIAN HOU TEMPLE

Taoism and Taoist temples in California are discussed in "*Three Chinese Temples in California: Marysville, Oroville, Weaverville* by Chuimei Ho and Bennet Bronson. Tong violence on Waverley Place is described in Richard H. Dillon's *The Hatchet Men: The Story of the Tong Wars in San Francisco's Chinatown*; Curt Gentry recounts the careers of Belle Cora and Ah Toy in *The Madams of San Francisco*. The description of Pike/Waverley as haunted by worn-out prostitutes in the 1870s is found in *Lights and Shades in San Francisco* by B. F. Lloyd. The tale of escaping from a Grant Avenue apartment through a back door onto Waverley is from *China 2227: Long, Long Ago* by Lyle Jan. Chinatown's post-quake architecture is the subject of *San Francisco Chinatown: A Guide to Its History and Architecture* by Philip P. Choy. The waning power of the tongs, and the political and economic power shift in Chinatown after 1906, is discussed in Ivan Light's "From Vice District to Tourist Attraction: The Moral Career of American Chinatowns 1880–1940," which appeared in the August 1974 *Pacific Historical Review*, and in the November 1974 edition of the same journal, "Conflict and the Web of Group Affiliation in San Francisco's Chinatown 1850–1910" by Stanford M. Lyman. The Golden Dragon massacre is discussed in *Chinatown Squad: Policing the Dragon From the Gold Rush to the 21st Century* by Kevin J. Mullen, and in much greater detail on the website Bamboo Tigers by Brockman Morris (http://brockmorris. com/btigers/index.html).

# CHAPTER FIVE: CALHOUN TERRACE

The saga of the Gray brothers is recounted in contemporaneous news accounts. "Doc" Robinson is discussed in *The San Francisco Stage: From Gold Rush to Golden Spike, 1849–1869* by Misha Berson. *The Farallon Islands: Sentinels of the Golden Gate* by Peter White gives an account of the Farallones Egg War. The hijinks at the Compound, the Hill's impoverished early days, and the fact that streets all over the world are paved with its rocks are described in David Myrick's *San Francisco's Telegraph Hill*. The Frank Norris quotation is from the essay "Among Cliff-Dwellers," which appeared in the magazine *The Wave* in May 1897.

## CHAPTER SIX: LOMBARD STREET

*Russian Hill: A History* by Edward F. Bielski provides accounts of the Dobson Observatory, the Hearst home, and the career of Carl Henry. The story of Humphrey's Castle is related in a 2012 piece in the Hidden History series by Alex Bevk, on the website SFCurbed. (https://sf.curbed.com/2012/9/24/10325420/pioneer-house-gave-early-glimpse-into-preservation-efforts).

The early history of Russian Hill is recounted in *Russian Hill: The Summit 1853–1906* by William Kostura. Hettie Belle Marcus's memoir of living on pre-curves Lombard Street is titled Lombard Street (https://archive.org/stream/histprojinterviews02julirich/histprojinterviews02julirich_djvu.txt).

## CHAPTER SEVEN: THE ROCK HOUSE

Doris Sloan's *Geology of the San Francisco Bay Region* provides an introduction to the rocks of San Francisco. The tale of the rock on Delta Street marking the spot where a group of Spanish soldiers got lost in 1777 is from "San Francisco's Visitacion Valley" by the Visitacion Valley History Project (Cynthia Cox et al.). The history of the Rock House was unearthed from various sources, including the Sanborn insurance maps in the San Francisco Public Library History Room, city directories, *On the Edge of the World: Four Architects in San Francisco at the Turn of the Century* by Richard Longstreth, *Arequipa Sanatorium: Life in California's Lung Resort for Women* by Lynn Downey, *San Francisco State University* by Meredith Eliassen, and "A Life by Design" by Robert de Roos, a feature on Rudolph Schaeffer that appeared in the April 22, 1979 edition of *California Living* magazine.

## CHAPTER EIGHT: HUNTINGTON PARK

The history of the Fontana delle Tartarughe is taken from Wikipedia. The career of Denis Kearney is dealt with in many sources, including *The Indispensable Enemy: Labor and the Anti-Chinese Movement in California* by Alexander Saxton; *San Francisco 1865–1932: Politics, Power, and Urban Development* by William Issel and Robert W. Cherny; and *The Public City: The Political Construction of Urban Life in San Francisco, 1850–1900* by Philip J. Ethington.

# CHAPTER NINE: THE MUSIC CONCOURSE

Evelyn Wells's fictionalized, sui generis account of the fifteen or so years before the 1906 disaster is titled *Champagne Days of San Francisco*. The story of bandleader Fritz Scheel is told in Raymond Clary's *The Making of Golden Gate Park: The Early Years, 1865–1906*. The history of the 1894 Midwinter Fair is recounted in a piece by Woody LaBounty on the website Outside Lands (https://www.outside-lands.org/1894_midwinter_fair.php) and in *San Francisco's Midwinter Exposition* by William Lipsky. The story of the anthropological expeditions dispatched for Chicago's Columbian Exposition is from a September 14, 2005, article in the *Chicago Tribune*, "It Took a Village." The Bert Williams story is largely drawn from *Introducing Bert Williams: Burnt Cork, Broadway and the Story of America's First Black Star* by Camille F. Forbes.

# CHAPTER TEN: THE PALACE OF FINE ARTS

The 1915 World's Fair is the subject of Laura Acker's *San Francisco's Jewel City: The Panama-Pacific International Exposition of 1915* and Frank Morton Todd's official history, "The Story of the Fair" (https://catalog.hathitrust.org/Record/001515106). Both also discuss the Palace of Fine Arts. The material on Bernard Maybeck is drawn from *Bernard Maybeck: Visionary Architect* by Sally Woodbridge, *Bernard Maybeck: Artisan, Architect, Artist* by Kenneth H. Cardwell, and *Five California Architects* by Esther McCoy.

Maybeck's own 1915 book on the Palace is titled *Palace of Fine Arts and Lagoon*. The Désert de Retz is the subject of Diana Ketcham's *Le Désert de Retz: A Late Eighteenth-Century French Folly Garden*. The section on Strawberry Island was drawn from *San Francisco Waterfront: Report on Historical Cultural Resources* by Roger Olmsted, Nancy Olmsted, and Allen Pastron; *San Francisco's Marina District* by William Lipsky; Gerald Robert Dow's MA thesis, "Bay Fill in San Francisco: A History of Change"; and Joel Pomerantz's *Seep City Sampler and Atlas*. R. P. Clark's essay on Harbor View is in *From Land's End to the Ferry*, ed. C. L. Camp. The story of the wild strawberry excursion in Yerba Buena is told in *75 Years in California* by William Heath Davis. Information on Yelamu sites in San Francisco was obtained by author interviews with historian Randall Milliken and Paul Scolari, American Indian liaison for the National Park Service in San Francisco. The Yelamu are discussed in "Ohlone/Costanoan Indians of the San

Francisco Peninsula and Their Neighbors, Yesterday and Today" by Randall Milliken, Laurence H. Shoup, and Beverly R. Ortiz. The early history of the area around the Harbor View Baths, and the story of the Bay Shore and Fort Point Road, are discussed in Robert Bardell's "The Presidio Road," which appeared in the winter 2012 issue of *The Argonaut*. The history of the Harbor View earthquake shacks is related in the San Francisco Relief Survey (https://www.russellsage.org/publications/san-francisco-relief-survey) and *Saving San Francisco: Relief and Recovery After the 1906 Disaster* by Andrea Rees Davies.

## CHAPTER ELEVEN: THE ALEMANY HEALTH CENTER

Joe Eskenazi profiled the Excelsior in a September 16, 2014, article for the *SF Weekly*, "Ever Upward: The Excelsior, the Blue-Collar Soul of the City, Struggles to Keep It Real in San Francisco's Era of Make-Believe." The story of the Emergency Hospital Service and the Alemany Health Center are drawn from the Landmark Designation Case Report for 35-45 Onandaga for the SF Planning Commission (https://commissions.sfplanning.org/hpcpackets/2015-003877DES.pdf ); "The History of the Surgical Service at San Francisco General Hospital," by William Schecter et al.; and "Catastrophes, Epidemics and Neglected Diseases: San Francisco General Hospital and the Evolution of Public Care" by William Blaisdell and Moses Grossman. The story of land grants to Californios in the Mexican era is found in Hubert Bancroft's *History of California*, Volumes 3 and 4; José Noé's petition for land is discussed in *Rancho San Miguel: A San Francisco Neighborhood History* by Mae Silver. The dispossession of the Californios is addressed by Leonard Pitt's *The Decline of the Californios: A Social History of the Spanish-Speaking Californians, 1846–1890*; the specific case of Rancho Buri-Buri, just south of San Francisco, is examined by Frank M. Stanger in "A California Rancho under Three Flags: A History of Rancho Buri Buri in San Mateo County," which appeared in the September 1938 issue of the *California Historical Quarterly*. The San Francisco and San Jose Railroad is discussed in *Bonanza Railroads* by Gilbert H. Kneiss. The priests' long commute from North Beach to say Mass is discussed in Walter G. Jebe Sr.'s *San Francisco's Excelsior District*.

# CHAPTER TWELVE: LANDS END

The material on Sutro Baths is drawn from *Sutro's Glass Palace: The Story of Sutro Baths* by John A. Martini, *Adolph Sutro: A Biography* by Robert E. Stewart Jr. and Mary F. Stewart, and *The San Francisco Cliff House* by Mary Germain Hountalas with Sharon Silva. The story of Kit Hing Hui was extensively covered in the *San Francisco Chronicle* and the *San Francisco Examiner*. The scenic Lands End steam engine route operated by the Ferries and Cliff House Railway is discussed on the *Outside Lands* podcast #320, with Woody LaBounty and David Gallagher, co-founders of the Western Neighborhoods Project (https://www.outsidelands. org/podcast/WNP320_Ferries_Cliff_RR). The story of Rivera's 1774 expedition to San Francisco is related in Alan K. Brown's *With Anza to California: The Journal of Pedro Font, O.F.M.* and in *San Francisco Bay: Discovery and Colonization, 1769–1776* by Theodore E. Treutlein. The material on the Mile Rocks Lighthouse is mostly drawn from *Guardians of the Golden Gate: Lighthouses and Lifeboat Stations of San Francisco Bay* by Ralph Shanks with Lisa Woo Shanks, editor.

# CHAPTER THIRTEEN: THE HAAS-LILIENTHAL HOUSE

Works on the history of Jews in San Francisco include *Cosmopolitans: A Social and Cultural History of the Jews of the San Francisco Bay Area* and *Visions of Reform: Congregation Emanu-El and the Jews of San Francisco, 1849–1999* by Fred Rosenbaum; *Our City: The Jews of San Francisco* by Irena Narell; *Pioneer Jews: A New Life in the Far West* by Harriet and Fred Rochlin; *920 O'Farrell Street: A Jewish Girlhood in Old San Francisco* by Harriet Lane Levy; and the film *American Jerusalem*, directed and written by Marc Shaffer. The story of the Reckendorfers is related in *Towers of Gold: How One Jewish Immigrant Named Isaias Hellman Created California* by Frances Dinkelspiel. *The Haas Sisters of Franklin Street: A Look Back with Love* by Frances Bransten Rothmann describes life in the Haas-Lilienthal house. The Haas-Lilienthal House website has more information on the house and its inhabitants (https://www.haas-lilienthalhouse.org/). Works on Victorian architecture include *In the Victorian Style* by Randolph Delehanty and Richard Sexton; *The Great Houses of San Francisco* by Thomas Aidala with photographs by Curt Bruce; *Victoria's Legacy: Tours of San Francisco Bay Area Architecture* by Judith Lynch Waldhorn and Sally B. Woodbridge; *Victorian Glory in San Francisco and the Bay Area* by Paul Duchscherer and Douglas Keister; and

*Victorian Classics of San Francisco*, a reissue of an 1888 series called *Artistic Homes of California*. The William Saroyan quotation is from his introduction to *San Francisco: West Coast Metropolis* by Edwin Rosskam.

## CHAPTER FOURTEEN: SHIPLEY STREET

The story of the three Indians weeping on the shore of Mission Bay is related in Hubert Bancroft's History of California, Volume 1. Mission Bay and its wetlands are discussed in *Vanished Waters: A History of San Francisco's Mission Bay*, by Nancy Olmsted. The subsidence of the reclaimed wetlands is described in *Down By the Bay: San Francisco's History Between the Tides* by Matthew Morse Booker; John Hittell's *A History of San Francisco and Incidentally of the State of California* discusses the Mission Plank Road. Russ's Gardens are discussed in "Men and Memories," op. cit., and in *The Annals of San Francisco* by Frank Soulé, John H. Gihon, and James Nisbet. The official report on the earthquake is "The California Earthquake of April 18, 1906" by Andrew C. Lawson et al. Accounts of the devastation around Sixth and Howard are found in "San Francisco Is Burning: The Untold Story of the 1906 Earthquake and Fire" by Dennis Smith and *Disaster! The Great San Francisco Earthquake and Fire of 1906* by Dan Kurzman. The author's firsthand account of the 1989 quake is from *Cool Gray City of Love: 49 Views of San Francisco*. The effect of the 1906 earthquake on ground throughout San Francisco is addressed by *Historic Ground Failures in Northern California Triggered by Earthquakes* by T. L. Youd and S. N. Hoose. The subsidence of Shipley Street and surrounding streets is discussed in Doris Sloan's *Geology of the San Francisco Bay Region*. A geological and historical walking tour of the area is provided by "Retracing the Events of the 1906 Earthquake and Fire Along the Old Bay Margins of Downtown San Francisco," by Raymond Sullivan (online), which includes a photograph of the patch of wetlands on Clara Street before it was built over.

## CHAPTER FIFTEEN: INA COOLBRITH PARK

The goat trail to the summit of Russian Hill and the Bohemian colony are discussed in "Russian Hill: The Summit" (op. cit.); "Russian Hill: A History" (op. cit.) provides additional history. Pedro Font's map is included in *Yerba Buena/ San Francisco: From the Beginning to the Gold Rush, 1769–1849*, compiled and edited by Peter Browning. The Rezanov-Arguello love story is related in *Glorious*

*Misadventures: Nikolai Rezanov and the Dream of a Russian America* by Owen Matthews. The speculation that Russian Hill was named for the dead Russian sailor is in *Historic Walks in San Francisco: 18 Trails Through the City's Past* by Rand Richards. The story of the polluted well is from John Henry Brown's *Reminiscences and Incidents of "the Early Days" of San Francisco*. Gelett Burgess is discussed in *Literary San Francisco: A Pictorial History from Its Beginnings to the Present Day* by Lawrence Ferlinghetti and Nancy J. Peters, in Oscar Lewis's *Bay Window Bohemia: The Brilliant Artistic World of Gaslit San Francisco*, and in Burgess's memoir *Bayside Bohemia: Fin de Siècle San Francisco and Its Little Magazines*.

## CHAPTER SIXTEEN: SOUTH PARK

The material on George Gordon is drawn from *A San Francisco Scandal: The California of George Gordon, Forty-Niner, Pioneer, and Builder of South Park* by Albert Shumate. South Park is discussed in Shumate's *Rincon Hill and South Park* (op. cit.); the latter work and Hittell (op. cit.) discuss the Second Street Cut. The earthquake tenements are described in the San Francisco Relief Survey (op. cit.). The *San Francisco Chronicle* reported extensively on the settlement house movement.

# INDEX

Note: *Italic* page numbers refer to illustrations.

## A NOTE ON THE AUTHOR AND ARTIST

**GARY KAMIYA** is the author of the number one San Francisco bestseller *Cool Gray City of Love: 49 Views of San Francisco*, which won the 2013 Northern California Book Award for creative nonfiction. His history column, Portals of the Past, has appeared for the past seven years in the *San Francisco Chronicle*. He was a cofounder and longtime executive editor of *Salon* and the former executive editor of *San Francisco* magazine. He lives on Telegraph Hill in San Francisco.

**PAUL MADONNA** is an award-winning artist and author. His popular series All Over Coffee ran in the *San Francisco Chronicle* for twelve years and has been collected into two sui generis bestsellers, *All Over Coffee* and *Everything is its own reward*. Paul is the creator of the Emit Hopper Mystery Series, and his unique brand of combining images and stories has been heralded as "an all new art form," celebrated internationally in galleries and museums as well as in print.